ARISE

ARISE
Communicate with Competence

General English
SEMESTER III & IV

The Department of English
Auxilium College (Autonomous),
Vellore

B L O O M S B U R Y
NEW DELHI • LONDON • OXFORD • NEW YORK • SYDNEY

BLOOMSBURY INDIA
Bloomsbury Publishing India Pvt. Ltd
Second Floor, LSC Building No. 4, DDA Complex,
Pocket C – 6 & 7, Vasant Kunj,
New Delhi 110070

First published in India 2025
This edition published in 2025

ISBN: 978-93-69521-42-5
2 4 6 8 10 9 7 5 3 1

Printed and bound in India by Gopsons Papers Pvt. Ltd.; Noida

To find out more about our authors and books, visit
www.bloomsbury.com and sign up for our newsletters

Contents

Foreword vii
Preface ix
Introduction xi
Contributors xiii

SEMESTER III

1. The Forty Fortunes: A Tale of Iran 3
   Aaron Shepard
2. If 10
   Rudyard Kipling
3. The Selfish Giant 13
   Oscar Wilde
4. Telephone Conversation 18
   Wole Soyinka
5. The Dear Departed 23
   Stanley Houghton
6. The Gift of the Magi 41
   O' Henry
7. On the Love of Life 47
   William Hazlitt
8. Nobel Prize Acceptance Speech 52
   Wangari Maathai
9. Of Friendship 60
   Francis Bacon

10. Leisure 67
W. H. Davies
11. Anxiety Monster 69
Rhona McFerran
12. On the Rule of the Road 72
A. G. Gardiner
13. And Still I Rise 79
Maya Angelou

SEMESTER IV

1. We Real Cool 85
Gwendolyn Brooks
2. Atomic Habits: Chapter 2 88
James Clear
3. The Giant's Wife: A Tall Tale of Ireland 100
William Carleton
4. Pride 107
Dahlia Ravikovitch
5. New Words for New Years 109
Shashi Tharoor
6. Angels and Blueberries 113
Tara Campbell
7. Dreams 117
Langston Hughes
8. Letters from a Father to His Daughter 119
Jawaharlal Nehru
9. Why I Write 122
George Orwell
10. Kabuliwala 131
Rabindranath Tagore
11. The Princess and the God: A Tale of Ancient India 140
Aaron Shepard
12. The Aged Mother 146
Matsuo Basho
13. The Quality of Mercy 150
William Shakespeare

Foreword

This General English Textbook, *Arise*, is thoughtfully designed to meet the academic and communicative needs of students. English, as a global language, continues to play a vital role in education, employment, and intercultural exchange. The ability to use it effectively has become an essential skill in today's interconnected world, enabling individuals to express themselves clearly, think critically, and engage meaningfully with people across cultures and disciplines.

This textbook aims to strengthen the foundational language skills of reading, writing, listening, and speaking, while also nurturing an appreciation for literature and creativity. The carefully selected lessons—ranging from timeless classics to modern writings—reflect diverse themes and experiences that broaden the learner's perspective.

Language teaching is not just about mastering rules; it is about developing confidence, clarity, and compassion in communication. Each unit of this book has been prepared with this philosophy in mind. It encourages learners not only to understand the text but also to connect it with their own lives, thoughts, and emotions. The exercises at the end of each lesson promote reflection, collaboration, and critical engagement.

This General English Textbook follows the TANSCHE syllabus, thoughtfully adapted and enhanced to suit the academic needs and learning context of our students at Auxilium College (Autonomous). The lessons prescribed for study provide greater relevance, inclusivity, and engagement, ensuring that learners receive both linguistic competence and cultural enrichment.

We believe that education is not just the acquisition of knowledge—it should nurture the whole person: intellect, imagination, and integrity. This *General English Textbook* reflects that vision. It aims to make students not only proficient users of language but also sensitive readers and thoughtful human beings capable of responding to the world with empathy and awareness.

I extend my heartfelt appreciation to the Department of English for their tireless efforts, scholarly insight, and dedication in preparing this volume. Their contribution has ensured that the textbook is both academically sound and pedagogically engaging. I appreciate all those who supported the editorial and publication process with care and commitment.

It is my sincere hope that this textbook will serve as a valuable resource for our students, guiding them toward excellence in language, thought, and expression. May it inspire them to use the power of words to build bridges of understanding and to contribute meaningfully to society.

Dr. (Sr.) Mary Josephine Rani
Secretary
Auxilium College (Autonomous), Vellore

Preface

This General English Textbook is based on the TANSCHE-prescribed syllabus, carefully modified to better serve the needs of our students at Auxilium College (Autonomous), Vellore. The purpose of this adaptation is not only to retain the academic framework provided by TANSCHE but also to make the material more meaningful, relatable, and engaging for our learners.

Language learning must evolve in response to the changing demands of education and society. While the original TANSCHE text provides a strong foundation, our faculty members have restructured certain lessons and added new ones to create a more balanced and inclusive learning experience. The content has been refined to emphasize practical communication skills, critical reading, and creative expression — areas that are vital for the holistic development of students in today's academic environment.

This edition reflects the belief that language learning is not confined to textbooks alone; it is an active process that connects classroom experience with real-life application. The revised lessons have been selected for their thematic depth, cultural value, and relevance to contemporary learners.

In an era shaped by Artificial Intelligence and digital transformation, the role of language learning has become even more vital. While technology can generate information, only human beings can give it meaning through empathy, creativity, and expression. The study of English thus equips students with the ability to think critically, communicate authentically, and strike a balance between technological advancement and human understanding. It helps learners use AI responsibly—seeing it not as a replacement for thought, but as a tool to enhance communication and learning.

Through this adapted version, we seek to offer students a textbook that is both academically challenging and intellectually stimulating. We hope that this edition will help them appreciate English not only as a language of study but as a medium for self-expression, creativity, and understanding.

The effort behind this revision is a reflection of our college's ongoing commitment to quality education. I sincerely commend the Faculty of the Department of English for their careful review, academic insight, and dedication in shaping this book into its present form.

This volume stands as a collaborative achievement—one that bridges institutional guidance, faculty innovation, and student-centred learning. May it serve its purpose well and inspire every learner to approach English with curiosity, confidence, and joy.

Dr. (Sr.) Arockia Jayaceli,
Principal
Auxilium College (Autonomous), Vellore

Introduction

The book *Arise: Communicate with Confidence*, a General English textbook for Semesters III and IV, is a collection of poems, short stories, fables, one-act plays, essays, and speeches, along with exercises designed to enhance the language skills of undergraduate students based on the syllabus prescribed by TANSCHE.

The chosen literary texts for study are simple, interesting, and insightful, providing an opportunity to get acquainted with other cultures through stories and poems. The chosen literary texts are significant and offer a platform to learn a language effectively. The literary texts are best suited for learners to acquire the much-needed 21st-century skills and social skills. The learners who identify themselves with the characters learn to be empathetic. The texts will stimulate critical thinking and to share ideas, which can help build communication skills. Literature enhances the lives of learners as they acquire a sense of hope and fulfilment. Literary texts can boost the confidence of the learners and encourage them to achieve more through mastering the language skills. Reading texts of different timelines can be challenging but it will inspire them to achieve their goals. The language of literature differs widely from everyday usage, but it can still make sense to the learners to explore the nuances of language.

The learners will be exposed to a wide range of activities such as vocabulary building, interpretation and critical analysis.

The exercises are designed to impart the four essential skills of listening, speaking, reading and writing. It can also spark creativity and enhance proficiency in speaking and writing skills. The main emphasis of the exercises designed for study is on the acquisition and use of language in varied contexts.

The core benefit of the learner acquiring proficiency in a language is that they gain confidence to perform well in their own domain of study. The general English textbook will be a beneficial tool for developing language through literature, enhancing the learner's communicative competence, and gaining transferable skills in view of career prospects. The textbook is best suited to help the learner use the English language more effectively and is a source of creating interest in lifelong learning.

Dr. (Sr.) Amala Valarmathy A.
Head of the Department – Vice Principal

Contributors

Department of English
(Auxilium College, Autonomous, Gandhinagar, Vellore)

- **Ms. Devanayagi A.**, M.A., M.Phil., SET, NET, (Ph.D), Asst. Prof.
- **Dr. Latha E.**, M.A., Ph.D., Asst.Prof.
- **Dr. Geetha R.**, M.A., M.Phil., B.Ed., Ph.D., Asst.Prof.
- **Ms. Gayathri R.**, M.A., M.Phil ., (Ph.D)., B.Ed., Asst. Prof.
- **Ms. Anitha Daisy Winfred**, M.A., NET., (Ph.D.), Asst. Prof.
- **Ms. Janani U.**, M.A., M.Phil, NET. (Ph.D) Asst. Prof.
- **Dr. Chitralekha D.**, M.A., M.Phil, SET., Ph.D., Asst. Prof.
- **Dr. Nisha K.A.**, M.A., B.Ed., M.Phil., Ph.D., Ast. Prof.
- **Ms. Griffa E.J.**, M.A., NET., (Ph.D.), Asst. Prof.
- **Dr. Sangamitra B.**, M.A., M.Phil, Ph.D., Asst Prof.
- **Ms. Isvarya P.**, M.A., M.Phil., NET., Asst. Prof.
- **Dr. Janice Sandra David**, M.A., Ph.D., Asst. Prof.
- **Dr. Caroline Unnathamani**, K., M.A., M.Phil., Ph.D., Asst. Prof.

SEMESTER III

The Forty Fortunes: A Tale of Iran

Aaron Shepard

Once, in the royal city of Isfahan, there lived a young man named Ahmed, who had a wife named Jamell. He knew no special craft or trade, but he had a shovel and a pick—and as he often told his wife, "If you can dig a hole, you can always earn enough to stay alive."

That was enough for Ahmed. But it was not enough for Jamell.

One day, as she often did, Jamell went to the public bath to wash herself in the hot pool and chat with the other women. But at the entrance, the woman in charge told her, "You can't come in now. The wife of the King's Royal Diviner is taking the whole place for herself."

"Who does she think she is?" protested Jamell. "Just because her husband tells fortunes!" But all she could do was return home, fuming all the way.

That evening, when Ahmed handed her his wages for the day, she said, "Look at these few measly coins! I won't put up with this any longer. Tomorrow you'll sit in the marketplace and be a diviner!"

"Jamell, are you insane?" said Ahmed. "What do I know about fortunetelling?"

"You don't need to know a thing," said Jamell. "When anyone brings you a question, you just throw the dice and mumble something that sounds wise. It's either that, or I go home to the house of my father!"

So the next day, Ahmed sold his shovel and his pick and bought the dice and the board and the robe of a fortuneteller. Then he sat in the marketplace near the public bath.

Hardly had he gotten settled when there ran up to him the wife of one of the King's ministers.

"Diviner, you must help me! I wore my most precious ring to the bath today, and now it's missing. Please, tell me where it is!"

Ahmed gulped and cast the dice. As he desperately searched for something wise to say, he happened to glance up at the lady's cloak. There he spied a small hole, and showing through the hole, a bit of her naked arm.

Of course, this was quite improper for a respectable lady, so Ahmed leaned forward and whispered urgently, "Madam, I see a hole."

"A what?" asked the lady, leaning closer.

"A hole! A hole!"

The lady brightened. "Of course! A hole!"

She rushed back to the bath and found the hole in the wall where she had hidden her ring for safekeeping and forgotten it. Then she came back out to Ahmed.

"God be praised!" she said. "You knew right where it was!" And to Ahmed's amazement, she gave him a gold coin.

That evening, when Jamell saw the coin and heard the story, she said, "You see? There's nothing to it!"

"God was merciful on this day," said Ahmed, "but I dare not test Him on another!"

"Nonsense," said Jamell. "If you want to keep your wife, you'll be back in the marketplace tomorrow."

Now, it happened that on that very night, at the palace of the King, the royal treasury was robbed. Forty pairs of hands carried away forty chests of gold and jewels.

The theft was reported next morning to the King. "Bring me my Royal Diviner and all his assistants," he commanded.

But though the fortunetellers cast their dice and mumbled quite wisely, not one could locate the thieves or the treasure.

"Frauds!" cried the King. "Throw them all in prison!"

Now, the King had heard about the fortuneteller who had found the ring of his minister's wife. So he sent two guards to the marketplace to bring Ahmed, who appeared trembling before him.

"Diviner," said the King, "my treasury has been robbed of forty chests. What can you tell me about the thieves?"

Ahmed thought quickly about forty chests being carried away. "Your Majesty, I can tell you there were . . . forty thieves."

"Amazing!" said the King. "None of my own diviners knew as much! But now you must find the thieves and the treasure."

Ahmed felt faint. "I'll . . . do my best, Your Majesty, but . . . but it will take some time."

"How long?" the King demanded.

"Uh . . . forty days, Your Majesty," said Ahmed, guessing the longest he could get. "One day for each thief."

"A long time indeed!" said the King. "Very well, you shall have it. If you succeed, I'll make you rich. If you don't, you'll rot with the others in prison!"

Back home, Ahmed told Jamell, "You see the trouble you have caused us? In forty days, the King will lock me away."

"Nonsense," said Jamell. "Just find the chests like you found the ring."

"I tell you, Jamell, I found nothing! That was only by the grace of God. But this time there's no hope."

Ahmed took some dried dates, counted out forty, and placed them in a jar. "I will eat one of these dates each evening. That will tell me when my forty days are done."

Now, it happened that one of the King's own servants was one of the forty thieves, and he had heard the King speak with Ahmed. That same evening, he hurried to the thieves' meeting place and reported to their chief. "There is a diviner who says he will find the treasure and the thieves in forty days!"

"He's bluffing," said the chief. "But we can't afford to take chances. Go to his house and find out what you can."

So the servant climbed up to the terrace on the flat roof of Ahmed's house, and he listened down the stairs that led inside. Just then, Ahmed took the first date from the jar and ate it. He told Jamell, "That's one."

The thief was so shocked, he nearly fell down the stairs. He hurried back to the meeting place and told the chief, "This diviner has amazing powers. Without seeing me, he knew I was on the roof! I clearly heard him say, 'That's one.'"

"You must have imagined it," said the chief. "Tomorrow night, two of you will go."

So the next night, the servant returned to Ahmed's roof with another of the thieves. As they were listening, Ahmed ate a second date and said, "That's two."

The thieves nearly tumbled over each other as they fled the roof and raced back to the chief. "He knew there were two of us!" said the servant. "We heard him say, 'That's two.'"

"It can't be!" said the chief. So the night after that, he sent three of the thieves, and the next night four, then five, then six.

And so it went till the fortieth night, when the chief said, "This time, I'll go with you myself." So all forty thieves climbed up to Ahmed's roof to listen.

Inside, Ahmed gazed at the last date in the jar, then sadly took it out and ate it. "That's forty. The number is complete."

Jamell sat beside him and gently took his hand. "Ahmed, during these forty days, I've been thinking. I was wrong to make you be a diviner. You are what you are, and I should not have tried to make you something else. Can you forgive me?"

"I forgive you, Jamell, but the fault is mine as well. I should not have done what I knew was not wise. But none of this helps us now."

Just then came a loud banging at the door.

Ahmed sighed. "The King's men already!" He went to the door and unbolted it, calling, "All right, all right, I know why you're here."

He swung the door open. To his astonishment, he saw forty men kneeling before him and touching their heads to the ground again and again.

"Of course, you know, O great diviner!" said the chief. "Nothing can be hidden from you. But we beg you not to give us away!"

Bewildered though he was, Ahmed realized that these must be the thieves. He thought fast and said, "Very well, I won't turn you in. But you must replace every bit of the treasure."

"At once! At once!" cried the chief.

And before the night was through, forty pairs of hands carried forty chests of gold and jewels back into the King's treasury.

Early the next morning, Ahmed appeared before the King. "Your Majesty, my magic arts can find either the treasure or the thieves, but not both. Which do you choose?"

"The treasure, I suppose," said the King, "though it's a pity not to get the thieves. The boiling oil is all ready for them. Well, never mind. Tell me where the treasure is, and I'll send my men right away."

"No need, Your Majesty." Ahmed waved his arms in the air and called, "Pish posh, wish wosh, mish mosh." Then he announced, "By my magic, the chests have returned to their place."

The King himself went with Ahmed to the treasury and found it so. "You are truly the greatest fortuneteller of the age!" he declared. "From this day forth, you shall be my Royal Diviner!"

"Thank you, Your Majesty," said Ahmed with a bow, "but I'm afraid that's impossible. Finding and restoring your treasure was so difficult, it used up all my powers. I shall never be a diviner again."

"What a loss!" cried the King. "Then I must doubly reward you. Here, take two of these chests for your own."

So Ahmed returned home to Jamell, safe, rich, and a good deal wiser. And as any diviner could have foretold, they lived happily ever after.

Exercise

The Forty Fortunes is a traditional Iranian folktale that tells the story of a poor man named Ahmed who accidentally finds a great fortune. Through a series of humorous and unexpected events he ends up gaining the king's favour and becoming wealthy. The story reflects themes of fate, luck, and the belief that kindness and honesty are ultimately rewarded. It offers readers a glimpse into Persian storytelling and cultural values.

A. Vocabulary Quest

- Rearrange the letters to form meaningful words.
- Identify the parts of speech (noun, verb, adjective, etc.)
- Write a sentence using the word in connection with *The Forty Fortunes.*

No.	*Jumbled Word*	*Answer*	*Parts of Speech*	*Sentence*
I	SROFTNEU	FORTUNES	Noun	Ahmed pretended to tell people's fortunes in the market.
II	VDENRII			
III	MEZETNAMA			
IV	VEOGIRF			
V	EPURTIITOUSSS			
VI	TSHEEIV			

B. Prepare a news story based on the report of an incident from *The Forty Fortunes.*

Anchor: "Good evening, citizens of Isfahan. In a shocking incident at the royal palace, forty chests of gold and jewels have gone missing. Our correspondent Laila is live at the scene. Laila, what can you tell us?"

Reporter: "Thank you. The King is furious and has imprisoned all his diviners. In a surprising turn, a common man named Ahmed, recently turned fortune teller, has claimed he can solve the case in forty days."

Eyewitness: "I saw the thieves last night sneaking out of the treasury. It was terrifying!"

Anchor: "Stay tuned for more updates on this developing story."

Suggested News Topics:

- Royal Treasury Robbed! Forty Chests Missing!
- Mysterious Diviner Stuns the King!
- Thieves Return Treasure Overnight!
- Ahmed, the Fortune teller Becomes a Hero!
- King Rewards Commoner with Two Treasure Chests!

C. Collect a few headlines from a regional language news of your choice and give alternate headlines in English.

If

Rudyard Kipling

If you can keep your head when all about you
Are losing theirs and blaming it on you,
If you can trust yourself when all men doubt you,
But make allowance for their doubting too;
If you can wait and not be tired by waiting,
Or being lied about, don't deal in lies,
Or being hated, don't give way to hating,
And yet don't look too good, nor talk too wise:

If you can dream—and not make dreams your master;
If you can think—and not make thoughts your aim;
If you can meet with Triumph and Disaster
And treat those two impostors just the same;
If you can bear to hear the truth you've spoken
Twisted by knaves to make a trap for fools,
Or watch the things you gave your life to, broken,
And stoop and build 'em up with worn-out tools:

If you can make one heap of all your winnings
And risk it on one turn of pitch-and-toss,

And lose, and start again at your beginnings
    And never breathe a word about your loss;
If you can force your heart and nerve and sinew
    To serve your turn long after they are gone,
And so hold on when there is nothing in you
    Except the Will which says to them: 'Hold on!'
If you can talk with crowds and keep your virtue,
    Or walk with Kings—nor lose the common touch,
If neither foes nor loving friends can hurt you,
    If all men count with you, but none too much;
If you can fill the unforgiving minute
    With sixty seconds' worth of distance run,
Yours is the Earth and everything that's in it,
    And—which is more—you'll be a Man, my son!

Exercise

If is an inspirational poem that provides advice about the values and principles that one should uphold in life. The poem provides various ways in which to rise above misfortune and emphasizes self-control, integrity, and perseverance in the face of adversity, advising the reader to remain composed, trust their own judgment, and treat both triumph and disaster with equanimity.

Write down three points revealing your wish:

If I were a Fairy...		If I were a wild animal...	
1.		1.	
2.		2.	
3.		3.	

If I were a writer...		If I were in space...	
1.		1.	
2.		2.	
3.		3.	

If I were a senior chef…		If I were the Head of My Family…	
1.		1.	
2.		2.	
3.		3.	

If I had lots of money…		If I had no money…	
1.		1.	
2.		2.	
3.		3.	

The Selfish Giant

Oscar Wilde

Every afternoon, as they were coming from school, the children used to go and play in the Giant's Garden.

It was a large lovely garden, with soft green grass. Here and there over the grass stood beautiful flowers like stars, and there were twelve peach-trees that in the spring-time broke out into delicate blossoms of pink and pearl, and in the autumn bore rich fruit. The birds sat on the trees and sang so sweetly that the children used to stop their games in order to listen to them. "How happy we are here!" they cried to each other.

One day the Giant came back. He had been to visit his friend the Cornish ogre, and had stayed with him for seven years. After the seven years were over he had said all that he had to say, for his conversation was limited, and he determined to return to his own castle. When he arrived he saw the children playing in the garden.

"What are you doing here?" he cried in a very gruff voice, and the children ran away.

"My own garden is my own garden," said the Giant; "anyone can understand that, and I will allow nobody to play in it but myself." So, he built a high wall all round it, and put up a notice-board.

Trespassers will be Prosecuted

He was a very selfish Giant.

The poor children had now nowhere to play. They tried to play on the road, but the road was very dusty and full of hard stones, and they did not like it. They used to wander round the high wall when their lessons were over, and talk about the beautiful garden inside. "How happy we were there," they said to each other.

Then the Spring came, and all over the country there were little blossoms and little birds. Only in the garden of the Selfish Giant it was still winter. The birds did not care to sing in it as there were no children, and the trees forgot to blossom. Once a beautiful flower put its head out from the grass, but when it saw the notice-board it was so sorry for the children that it slipped back into the ground again, and went off to sleep. The only people who were pleased were the Snow and the Frost. "Spring has forgotten this garden," they cried, "so we will live here all the year round." The Snow covered up the grass with her great white cloak, and the Frost painted all the trees silver. Then they invited the North Wind to stay with them, and he came. He was wrapped in furs, and he roared all day about the garden, and blew the chimney-pots down. "This is a delightful spot," he said, "we must ask the Hail on a visit." So the Hail came. Every day for three hours he rattled on the roof of the castle till he broke most of the slates, and then he ran round and round the garden as fast as he could go. He was dressed in grey, and his breath was like ice.

"I cannot understand why the Spring is so late in coming," said the Selfish Giant, as he sat at the window and looked out at his cold white garden; "I hope there will be a change in the weather."

But the Spring never came, nor the Summer. The Autumn gave golden fruit to every garden, but to the Giant's Garden she gave none. "He is too selfish," she said. So it was always Winter there, and the North Wind, and the Hail, and the Frost, and the Snow danced about through the trees.

One morning the Giant was lying awake in bed when he heard some lovely music. It sounded so sweet to his ears that he thought it must be the King's musicians passing by.

It was really only a little linnet singing outside his window, but it was so long since he had heard a bird sing in his garden that it seemed to him to be the most beautiful music in the world. Then the Hail stopped dancing over his head, and the North Wind ceased roaring, and a delicious perfume came to him through the open casement. "I believe the Spring has come at last," said the Giant; and he jumped out of bed and looked out.

What did he see?

He saw a most wonderful sight. Through a little hole in the wall the children had crept in, and they were sitting in the branches of the trees. In every tree that he could see there was a little child. And the trees were so glad to have the children back again that they had covered themselves with blossoms, and were waving their arms gently above the children's heads. The birds were flying about and twittering with delight, and the flowers were looking up through the green grass and laughing. It was a lovely scene, only in one corner it was still winter. It was the farthest corner of the garden, and in it was standing a little boy. He was so small that he could not reach up to the branches of the tree, and he was wandering all round it, crying bitterly. The poor tree was still quite covered with frost and snow, and the North Wind was blowing and roaring above it. "Climb up! little boy," said the Tree, and it bent its branches down as low as it could; but the boy was too tiny.

And the Giant's heart melted as he looked out. "How selfish I have been!" he said; "now I know why the Spring would not come here. I will put that poor little boy on the top of the tree, and then I will knock down the wall, and my garden shall be the children's playground for ever and ever." He was really very sorry for what he had done.

So he crept downstairs and opened the front door quite softly, and went out into the garden. But when the children saw him they were so frightened that they all ran away, and the garden became winter again. Only the little boy did not run, for his eyes were so full of tears that he did not see the Giant coming. And the Giant stole up behind him and took him gently in his hand, and put him up into the tree. And the tree broke at once into blossom, and the birds came and sang on it, and the little boy stretched out his two arms and flung them round the Giant's neck, and kissed him. And the other children, when they saw that the Giant was not wicked any longer, came running back, and with them came the Spring. "It is your garden now, little children," said the Giant, and he took a great axe and knocked down the wall. And when the people were going to market at twelve o'clock, they found the Giant playing with the children in the most beautiful garden they had ever seen.

All day long they played, and in the evening, they came to the Giant to bid him good-bye.

"But where is your little companion?" he said: "the boy I put into the tree." The Giant loved him the best because he had kissed him.

"We don't know," answered the children; "he has gone away."

"You must tell him to be sure and come here to-morrow," said the Giant. But the children said that they did not know where he lived, and had never seen him before; and the Giant felt very sad.

Every afternoon, when school was over, the children came and played with the Giant. But the little boy whom the Giant loved was never seen again.

The Giant was very kind to all the children, yet he longed for his first little friend, and often spoke of him. "How I would like to see him!" he used to say.

Years went over, and the Giant grew very old and feeble. He could not play about any more, so he sat in a huge armchair, and watched the children at their games, and admired his garden. "I have many beautiful flowers," he said; "but the children are the most beautiful flowers of all."

One winter morning he looked out of his window as he was dressing. He did not hate the Winter now, for he knew that it was merely the Spring asleep, and that the flowers were resting.

Suddenly he rubbed his eyes in wonder, and looked and looked. It certainly was a marvelous sight. In the farthest corner of the garden was a tree quite covered with lovely white blossoms. Its branches were all golden, and silver fruit hung down from them, and underneath it stood the little boy he had loved.

Downstairs ran the Giant in great joy, and out into the garden. He hastened across the grass, and came near to the child. And when he came quite close his face grew red with anger, and he said, "Who hath dared to wound thee?" For on the palms of the child's hands were the prints of two nails, and the prints of two nails were on the little feet.

"Who hath dared to wound thee?" cried the Giant; "tell me, that I may take my big sword and slay him."

"Nay!" answered the child; "but these are the wounds of Love."

"Who art thou?" said the Giant, and a strange awe fell on him, and he knelt before the little child.

And the child smiled on the Giant, and said to him, "You let me play once in your garden, to-day you shall come with me to my garden, which is Paradise."

And when the children ran in that afternoon, they found the Giant lying dead under the tree, all covered with white blossoms.

Exercise

The Selfish Giant is a moral tale about a giant who initially forbids children from playing in his garden, causing it to fall into permanent winter. When he realizes his mistake and welcomes the children back, the garden blooms again with joy. A special child later appears symbolizing divine love and redemption. The story highlights the importance of kindness, sharing, and transformation through love.

- **Role-Play**
  Write a skit in pairs or small groups with scenes depicting the Giant's initial selfishness and his eventual change of heart.
- **Diary Entries**
  Write a diary entry from the perspective of the Giant or one of the children. Explore their feelings about the Giant's transformation and the arrival of spring.
- **Rewrite the Ending**
  Imagine an alternative ending where the Giant remains selfish. Write a short paragraph describing how the story would unfold differently.

Telephone Conversation

Wole Soyinka

The price seemed reasonable, location
Indifferent. The landlady swore she lived
Off premises. Nothing remained
But self-confession. "Madam," I warned,
"I hate a wasted journey—I am African."
Silence. Silenced transmission of
Pressurized good-breeding. Voice, when it came,
Lipstick coated, long gold-rolled
Cigarette-holder pipped. Caught I was foully.
"HOW DARK?" . . . I had not misheard . . . "ARE YOU LIGHT
OR VERY DARK?" Button B, Button A.* Stench
Of rancid breath of public hide-and-speak.
Red booth. Red pillar box. Red double-tiered
Omnibus squelching tar. It was real! Shamed
By ill-mannered silence, surrender
Pushed dumbfounded to beg simplification.
Considerate she was, varying the emphasis--
"ARE YOU DARK? OR VERY LIGHT?" Revelation came.
"You mean—like plain or milk chocolate?"
Her assent was clinical, crushing in its light

Impersonality. Rapidly, wave-length adjusted,
I chose. "West African sepia"—and as afterthought,
"Down in my passport." Silence for spectroscopic
Flight of fancy, till truthfulness clanged her accent
Hard on the mouthpiece. "WHAT'S THAT?" conceding
"DON'T KNOW WHAT THAT IS." "Like brunette."
"THAT'S DARK, ISN'T IT?" "Not altogether.
Facially, I am brunette, but, madam, you should see
The rest of me. Palm of my hand, soles of my feet
Are a peroxide blond. Friction, caused—
Foolishly, madam—by sitting down, has turned
My bottom raven black—One moment, madam!"—sensing
Her receiver rearing on the thunderclap
About my ears—"Madam," I pleaded, "wouldn't you rather
See for yourself?"

Exercise

The poem *Telephone Conversation* explores the theme of racism through a powerful yet ironic exchange between an African man and a white landlady over the phone. The poem begins with the man inquiring about renting an apartment, but the conversation takes a turn when the landlady asks about his skin color. The speaker responds with wit and sarcasm, highlighting the absurdity of judging someone based on race. Through clever language, humor, and a satirical tone, Wole Soyinka exposes the deep-rooted prejudice in society. The poem is both humorous and unsettling, forcing readers to reflect on the persistence of racism in everyday life.

I. Answer the following

Section A – Multiple Choice Questions:

1. Which of the following is NOT good telephone etiquette?

A. Speaking clearly
B. Interrupting the caller
C. Being polite and professional
D. Listening carefully

2. What should you do if you need to place a caller on hold?
   A. Just put them on hold without saying anything
   B. Say, "Hold on" and leave them waiting
   C. Ask politely, "May I place you on hold for a moment?"
   D. Hang up and call them back later
3. Which of these voice qualities is most important in phone etiquette?
   A. Volume, speed, clarity, and tone
   B. Accent
   C. Humor
   D. Whispering
4. How should you answer a professional phone call?
   A. "What do you want?"
   B. "Yeah, who is this?"
   C. "Hello, [Company Name], this is [Your Name]. How can I help you?"
   D. "Speak quickly, I'm busy."

Section B: True or False

1. Your tone of voice can affect how the caller perceives you.\
2. It's okay to eat or chew while speaking on the phone.
3. Smiling while speaking on the phone helps you sound more friendly.
4. If you don't know the answer to a caller's question, guess the answer.

Section C: Fill in the Blanks

1. Before ending the call, always say "________" to leave a polite impression.
   Answer: Thank you or Goodbye
2. If the caller is speaking too fast or unclear, you should politely ask them to ________.
   Answer: Repeat or Speak slowly

II. Chat App Dialogue

Imagine the conversation happening through **WhatsApp or Telegraph app**.

Example: "Hi! Is the room still available?"

III. Answer the Phone

Type: Role-play

(a) Write a phone call conversation – For example, One person is the **caller**; the other the **landlord/lady**.

Receptionist: Good afternoon. Riverdale Apartments. How can I help you?

Caller: Good afternoon. I'm calling to ask if the studio apartment on Hill Road is still
available.

Receptionist: Yes, it is. Would you like to schedule a visit?

Caller: Yes, please. I would like to see the place tomorrow morning, if possible.

Receptionist: Certainly. What time are you available?

Caller: Around 10 a.m. Will that work?

Receptionist: Let me check… Yes, that works perfectly. What's your full name, please?

Caller: My name is Samuel Okoro. That's O-K-O-R-O.

Receptionist: Thank you, Mr. Okoro. And may I ask, how did you hear about the apartment?

Caller: I saw the ad online. On a site called "QuickStay Rentals."

Receptionist: Great! When you arrive, please check in at the front desk. A staff member will show you around.

Caller: Perfect. One last question—does the rent include utilities?

Receptionist: Yes, it does. It also includes Wi-Fi and water.

Caller: That's good to know. Thank you for your help.

Receptionist: You're welcome! See you tomorrow at 10 a.m.

(b) **Convert the completed dialogue into Reported Speech.**

For example: Samuel asked if the studio apartment on Hill Road was still available.

The receptionist replied that it was...

(c) **Complete the Conversation based on Wole Soyinka's "Telephone Conversation"**

Landlady: Hello?

Speaker: Good afternoon. I'm calling about the room you __________ (advertise) for rent.

Landlady: Oh yes, it's still available. May I ask—what's your name?

Speaker: My name is not important right now. I thought I should let you know: I am African.

Landlady: Oh... I see. I hope you don't mind me __________ (ask) a few questions.

Speaker: Of course not. Please, go ahead.

Landlady: Well... I mean... are you ________ (light-skinned / dark-skinned)?

Speaker: Would you prefer I send a colour chart?

Landlady: No, no... I just mean, how _____________ (dark / are / you), exactly?

Speaker: My palms are _______________ (white / like / paper), my soles the same. But my face, my boto—well, they've had more sun.

Landlady: I see… (silence)

Speaker: Still there?

Landlady: Yes. I think... I'll call you back. (She hangs up.)

The Dear Departed

Stanley Houghton

(The scene is the sitting room of a small house in a lower middle-class district of a provincial town. On the spectator's left is the window, with the blinds down. A sofa is in front of it. On his right is a fireplace with an armchair by it. In the middle of the wall facing the spectator is the door into the passage. To the left of the door a cheap, shabby chest of drawers, to the right a sideboard. In the middle of the room is a table, with chairs round it. Ornaments and a cheap American clock are on the mantelpiece, in the hearth a kettle. By the sideboard a pair of gaudy new carpet slippers.

The table is partly laid for tea, and the necessaries for the meal are on the sideboard, as also are copies of an evening paper and of TIT-BITS and PEARSON'S WEEKLY. Turning to the left through the door takes you to the front door; to the right, up-stairs. In the passage a hatstand is visible. When the curtain rises Mrs. Slater is seen laying the table. She is a vigorous, plump, red-faced, vulgar woman, prepared to do any amount of straight talking to get her own way. She is in black, but not in complete mourning. She listens for a moment and then goes to the window, opens it and calls into the street.)

MRS. SLATER: (sharply) Victoria, Victoria! D'ye hear? Come in, will you?

(MRS. SLATER closes window and puts the blind straight and then returns to her work at the table. VICTORIA, a precocious girl often, dressed in colours, enters.)

MRS. SLATER: I'm amazed at you, Victoria; I really am. How you can gallivanting about in the street with your grandfather lying dead and cold upstairs, I don't know. Be off now, and change your dress before your Aunt Elizabeth and your Uncle Ben come. It would never do for them to find you in colours.

VICTORIA: What are they coming for? They haven't been here for ages.

MRS. SLATER: They're coming to talk over poor grandpa's affairs. Your father sent them a telegram as soon as we found he was dead. (*A noise is heard.*)

Good gracious, that's never them. (MRS. SLATER: hurries to the door and opens it.) No, thank goodness! It's only your father.

HENRY SLATER, a stooping, heavy man with a drooping moustache, enters. He is wearing a black tailcoat, grey trousers, a black lie and a bowler hat. He carriers a little paper parcel.

HENRY: Not come yet, eh?

MRS. SLATER: You can see they haven't, can't you? Now, Victoria, be off upstairs and that quick. Put your white frock on with a black sash.

(VICTORIA goes out.)

MRS. SLATER: (to HENRY): I'm not satisfied, but it's the best we can do till our new black's ready, and Ben and Elizabeth will never have thought about mourning yet, so we'll outshine them there-

(HENRY sits in the armchair by the fire.)

Get your boots off, HENRY; Elizabeth's that prying she notices the least speck of dirt.

HENRY: I'm wondering if they'll come at all. When you an Elizabeth quarreled she said she'd never set foot in your house again.

MRS. SLATER: She'll come fast enough after her share of what grandfather's left. You know how hard she can be when she likes. Where she gets it from I can't tell. (MRS. SLATER unwraps the parcel HENRY has brought. It contains an apple pie, which she puts on a dish on the table.)

HENRY: I suppose it's in the family.

MRS. SLATER: What do you mean by that. Henry Slater?

HENRY: I was referring to your father, not to you. Where are my slippers?

MRS. SLATER: In the kitchen; but you want a new pair, those old ones are nearly worn out. (Nearly breaking down.) You don't seem to realize what it's costing me to bear up like I am doing. My heart's fit to break when I see the little trifles that belonged to grandfather lying around, and think he'll never use them again. (Briskly)

Here! You'd better wear these slippers of grandfather's now. It's lucky he'd just got a new pair.

HENRY: They'll be very small for me, my dear.

MRS. SLATER: They'll stretch, won't they? I'm not going to have them wasted. (She has finished laying the table.)

Henry, I've been thinking about that bureau of grandfather's that's in his bedroom. You know I always wanted to have it after he died.

HENRY: You must arrange with Elizabeth when you're dividing things up.

MRS. SLATER: Elizabeth's that sharp she'll see I'm after it, and she'll drive a hard bargain over it. Eh, what it is to have a low money grubbing spirit!

HENRY: Perhaps she's got her eye on the bureau as well.

MRS. SLATER: She's never been here since grandfather bought it. If it was only down here instead of in his room, she'd never guess it wasn't our own.

HENRY: (startled) Amelia! (He rises.)

MRS. SLATER: Henry, why shouldn't we bring that bureau down here now? We could do it before they come.

HENRY (*stupefied*): I wouldn't care to.

MRS. SLATER: Don't look so daft. Why not?

HENRY: It doesn't seem delicate, somehow.

MRS. SLATER: We could put that shabby old chest of drawers upstairs where the bureau is now. Elizabeth could have that and welcome. I've always wanted to get rid of it. (She points to the drawers.)

HENRY: Suppose they come when we're doing it.

MRS. SLATER: I'll fasten the front door. Get your coat off. Henry; we'll change it.

(MRS. SLATE goes out to fasten the front door. HENRY takes his coat off. MRS. SLATE reappears.)

MRS. SLATER: I'll run up and move the chairs out of the way.

(VICTORIA appears, dressed according to her mother's instructions.)

VICTORIA: Will you fasten my frock up the back, mother?

MRS. SLATER: I'm busy; get your father to do it.

(MRS. SLATER: hurries upstairs, and HENRY fastens the frock.)

VICTORIA: What have you got your coat off for, Father?

HENRY: Mother and me is going to bring grandfather's bureau down here.

VICTORIA: (after a moment's thought.): Are we pinching it before Aunt Elizabeth comes?

HENRY: (shocked) No, my child. Grandpa gave it to your mother before he died.

VICTORIA: This morning?

HENRY: Yes.

VICTORIA: Ah! He was drunk this morning.

HENRY: Hush; you mustn't ever say he was drunk, now. (HENRY has fastened the frock, and MRS. SLATER appears carrying a handsome clock under her arm.)

MRS. SLATER: I thought I'd fetch this down as well. (She puts it on the mantelpiece.) Our clock's worth nothing and this always appealed to me.

VICTORIA: That's grandpa's clock.

MRS. SLATER: Chut! Be quit! It's ours now. Come Henry, lift your end. Victoria, don't breathe a word to your aunt about the clock and the bureau.

(They carry the chest of drawers through the doorway.)

VICTORIA: (to herself) I thought we'd pinched them.

(After a short pause there is a sharp knock at the front door.)

MRS. SLATER: (from upstairs) Victoria, if that's your aunt and uncle you're not to open the door.

(VICTORIA peeps through the window.)

VICTORIA: Mother, It's them.

MRS. SLATER: You're not to open the door till I come down. (Knocking repeated.)

Let them knock away. (There is a heavy bumping noise.)

Mind the wall. Henry. (HENRY and MRS. SLATER, very hot and flushed, stagger in with a pretty old-fashioned bureau containing a locked desk. They put it where the chest of drawers was, and straighten the ornaments, etc. The knocking is repeated.)

MRS. SLATER: That was a near thing. Open the door, Victoria. Now, Henry, get your coat on. (She helps him.)

HENRY: Did we knock much plaster off the wall?

MRS. SLATER: Never mind the plaster. Do I look all right? (Straightening her hair at the glass.) Just watch Elizabeth's face when she sees we're all in half-mourning. (Throwing him Tit-Bits.) Take this and sit down. Try and look as if we'd been waiting for them.

(HENRY sits in the armchair and MRS. SLATER left of table. They read ostentatiously. VICTORIA ushers in BEN and MRS. JORDAN. The latter is a stout, complacent woman with an impassive and an irritating air of being always right. She is wearing a complete and deadly outfit of new mourning crowned by a great black hat with plumes. BEN is also in complete new mourning, with black gloves and a band round his hat. He is rather a jolly little man, accustomed to be humorous, but at present trying to adapt himself to the regrettable occasion. He has a bright, chirpy little voice. BEN sails into the room and solemnly goes straight to MRS. SLATER and kisses her. The men shake hands. Not a word is spoken. MRS. SLATER furtively inspects the new mourning.)

MRS. JORDAN: Well, Amelia, and he's gone at last.

MRS. SLATER: Yes, he's gone. He was seventy-two a fortnight last Sunday. (She sniffs back a tear. MRS. JORDAN sits on the left of the table. MRS. SLATER on the right. HENRY in the armchair. BEN on the sofa with VICTORIA near him.)

BEN: (chirpily) Now, Amelia, you mustn't give way. We've all got to die some time or other. It might have been worse.

MRS. SLATER: I don't see how.

BEN: It might have been one of us.

HENRY: It's taken you a long time to get here, Elizabeth.

MRS. JORDAN: Oh, I couldn't do it. I really couldn't do it.

MRS. SLATER: (suspiciously) Couldn't do what?

MRS. JORDAN: I couldn't start without getting the mourning. (Glancing at her sister.)

MRS. SLATER: We've ordered ours, you may be sure. (Acidly) I never could fancy buying ready-made things.

MRS. JORDAN: No? For myself it's such a relief to get into the black. And now perhaps you'll tell us all about it. What did the doctor say?

MRS. SLATER: Oh, he's not been near yet.

MRS. JORDAN: Not been near?

BEN: (in the same breath) Didn't you send for him at once?

MRS. SLATER: Of course I did. Do you take me for a fool? I sent Henry at once for Dr. Pringle but he was out.

BEN: You should have gone for another. Eh, Eliza?

MRS. JORDAN: Oh, yes. It's a fatal mistake.

MRS. SLATER: Pringle attended him when he was alive and Pringle shall attend him when he's dead. That's professional etiquette.

BEN: Well, you know your own business best, but-

MRS. JORDAN: Yes-it's a fatal mistake.

MRS. SLATER: Don't talk so silly, Elizabeth. What good could a doctor have done?

MRS. JORDAN: Look at the many cases of persons being restored to life hours after they were thought to be 'gone'.

HENRY: That's when they've been drowned. Your father wasn't drowned, Elizabeth.

BEN: (humorously) There wasn't much fear of that. If there was one thing he couldn't bear, it was water. (He laughs, but no else does.)

MRS. JORDAN (pained): BEN!

(BEN is crushed at once.)

MRS. SLATER (piqued): I'm sure he washed regular enough.

MRS. JORDAN: If he did take a drop too much at times, we'll not dwell on that, now.

MRS. SLATER: Father had been 'merry' this morning. He went out soon after breakfast to pay his insurance.

BEN: My word, its a good thing he did.

MRS. JORDAN: He always was thoughtful in that way. He was too honourable to have 'gone' without paying his premium.

MRS. SLATER: Well, he must have gone round to the 'Ring-o'-Bells' afterwards, for he came in as merry as a sandboy. I says, 'We're only waiting for Henry to start dinner'. 'Dinner', he says 'I don't want no dinner. I'm going to bed!'

BEN: (shaking his head) Ah! Dear, dear.

HENRY: And when I came in I found him undressed sure enough and snug in bed. (He rises and stands on the hearthrug.)

MRS. JORDAN: (definitely)

Yes, he'd had a 'warning'. I'm sure of that. Did he know you?

HENRY: Yes. He spoke to me.

MRS. JORDAN: Did he say he'd had a 'warning'?

HENRY: No. He said, 'Henry, would you mind taking my boots off? I forgot before I got into bed'.

MRS. JORDAN: He must have been wandering.

HENRY: No, he'd got' em on all right.

MRS. SLATER: And when we'd finished dinner I thought I'd take up a bit of something on a tray. He was lying there for all the world as if he was asleep, so I put the tray down on the bureau – (correcting herself) on the chest of drawers – and went to waken him. (A pause.) He was quite cold.

HENRY: Then I heard Amelia calling for me, and I ran upstairs.

MRS. SLATER: Of course we could do nothing.

MRS. JORDAN: He was 'gone'?

HENRY: There wasn't any doubt.

MRS. JORDAN: I always knew he'd go sudden in the end.

(A pause. They – wipe their eyes and sniff back tears.)

MRS. SLATER: (rising briskly at length: in a business-like tone)

Well, will you go up and look at him now, or shall we have tea?

MRS. JORDAN: What do you say, Ben?

BEN: I'm not particular.

MRS. JORDAN: (surveying, the table) Well, then, if the kettle's ready we may as well have tea first.

(*MRS. SLATER puts the kettle on the fire and gets tea ready.)*

HENRY: One thing we may as well decide now; the announcement in the papers.

MRS. JORDAN: I was thinking of that. What would you put?

MRS. SLATER: At the residence of his daughter, 235 Upper Cornbank Street, etc.

HENRY: You wouldn't care for a bit of poetry?

MRS. JORDAN: I like 'Never Forgotten'. It's refined.

HENRY: Yes, but it's rather soon for that.

BEN: You couldn't very well have forgot him the day after.

MRS. SLATER: I always fancy, 'A loving husband, a kind father, and a faithful friend'.

BEN: (doubtfully) Do you think that's right?

HENRY: I don't think it matters whether it's right or not.

MRS. JORDAN: No, it's more for the look of the thing.

HENRY: I saw a verse in the Evening News yesterday. Proper poetry it was - it rhymed. (He gets the paper and reads.)

'Despised and forgotten by some you may be, But the spot that contains you is sacred to we.'

MRS. JORDAN: That'll never do. You don't say 'scared to we'.

HENRY: It's in the paper.

MRS. SLATER: You wouldn't say it if you were speaking properly, but it's different in poetry.

HENRY: Poetic license, you know.

MRS. JORDAN: No, that'll never do. We want a verse that says how much we loved him and refers to all his good qualities and says what a heavy loss we've had.

MRS. SLATER: You want a whole poem. That'll cost a good lot.

MRS. JORDAN: Well, we'll think about it after tea, and then we'll look through his bits of things and make a list of them. There's all the furniture in his room.

HENRY: There's no jewellery or valuables of that sort.

MRS. JORDAN: Except his gold watch. He promised that to our Jimmy.

MRS. SLATER: Promised to your Jimmy! I never heard of that.

MRS. JORDAN: Oh, but he did, Amelia, when he was living with us. He was very fond of Jimmy.

MRS. SLATER: Well. (Amazed.) I don't know!

BEN: Anyhow, there's his insurance money. Have you got the receipt for the premium he paid this morning?

MRS. SLATER: I've not seen it.

(VICTORIA, jumps up from the sofa and comes behind the table.)

VICTORIA: Mother, I don't think Grandpa went to pay his insurance this morning.

MRS. SLATER: He went out.

VICTORIA: Yes, but he didn't go into the town. He met old Mr. Tattersall down the street, and they went off past St. Philip's Church.

MRS. SLATER: To the 'Ring-o'-Bells', I'll be bound.

BEN: The -Ring-o'-Bells'?

MRS. SLATER: That public-house that John Shorrock's widow keeps. He is always hanging about there. Oh, if he hasn't paid it -

BEN: Do you think he hasn't paid it? Was it overdue?

MRS. SLATER: I should think it was overdue.

MRS. JORDAN: Something tells me he's not paid it. I've a 'warning', I know it; he's not paid it.

BEN: The drunken old beggar.

MRS. JORDAN: He's done it on purpose, Just to annoy us.

MRS. SLATER: After all I've done for him, having to put up with him in the house these three years. It's nothing short of swindling.

MRS. JORDAN: I had to put up with him for five years.

MRS. SLATER: And you were trying to turn him over to us all the time.

HENRY: But we don't know for certain that he's not paid the premium.

MRS. JORDAN: I do. It's come over me all at once that he hasn't.

MRS. SLATER: Victoria, run upstairs and fetch that bunch of keys that's on your grandpa's dressing table.

VICTORIA: (timidly) In Grandpa's room?

MRS. SLATER: Yes.

VICTORIA: I-I don't like to.

MRS. SLATER: Don't talk so silly. There's no one can hurt you. (VICTORIA goes out reluctantly.) We'll see if he's locked the receipt up in the bureau.

BEN: In where? In this thing? (He rises and examines it.)

MRS. JORDAN: (also rising)

Where did you pick that up, Amelia? It's new since last I was here.

(They examine it closely.)

MRS. SLATER: Oh-Henry picked it up one day.

MRS. JORDAN: I like it. It's artistic. Did you buy it at an auction?

HENRY: Eh! Where did I buy it, Amelia?

MRS. SLATER: Yes, at an auction.

BEN: (disparagingly) Oh, second-hand.

MRS. JORDAN: Don't show your ignorance, Ben. All artistic things are secondhand. Look at those old masters.

(VICTORIA returns, very scared. She closes the door after her.)

VICTORIA: Mother! Mother!

MRS. SLATER: What is it, child?

VICTORIA: Grandpa's getting up.

BEN: What?

MRS. SLATER: What do you say?

VICTORIA: Grandpa's getting up.

MRS. JORDAN: The child's crazy.

MRS. SLATER: Don't talk so silly. Don't you know your grandpa's dead?

VICTORIA: No, no; he's getting up. I saw him.

(They are transfixed with amazement. BEN and MRS. JORDAN left of table. VICTORIA clings to MRS. SLATER, right of table HENRY near fireplace.)

MRS. JORDAN: You'd better go up and see for yourself, Amelia.

MRS. SLATER: Here-come with me, Henry. (HENRY draws back terrified)

BEN: (suddenly)

Hist! Listen.

(They look at the door. A slight chuckling is heard outside. The door opens, revealing an old man clad in a faded but gay dressing-gown. He is in his stockinged feet. Although over seventy, he is

vigorous and well coloured; his bright, malicious eyes twinkle under his heavy, reddish-grey eyebrows. He is obviously either Grandfather ABEL MERRYWEATHER *or else his ghost.*)

ABEL: What's the matter with little Vicky? (He sees BEN and MRS. JORDAN); Hello! What brings you here? How's yourself, Ben? (*ABEL thrusts his hand at BEN, who skips back smartly and retreats to a safe distance below the sofa.*)

MRS. SLATER (approaching ABEL gingerly) Grandfather, is that you? (She pokes him with her hand to see if he is solid.)

ABEL: (irritated by the whispering) Of course it's me. Don't do that, 'Melia. What the devil do you mean by this tomfoolery?

MRS. SLATER: (to the others) He's not dead.

BEN: Doesn't seem like it.

ABEL: You've kept away long enough, Lizzie; and now you've come, you don't seem over-pleased to see me.

MRS. JORDAN: You took us by surprise, father. Are you keeping quite well?

ABEL: (trying to catch the words.) Eh? What?

MRS. JORDAN: Are you quite well?

ABEL: Aye, I'm right enough but for a bit of a headache. I wouldn't mind betting that I'm not the first in this house to be carried to the cemetery. I always think Henry there looks none too healthy.

MRS. JORDAN: Well, I never!

(ABEL crosses to the armchair, HENRY gets out of his way to the front of the table.)

ABEL: 'Melia, what the dickens did I do with my new slippers?

MRS. SLATER: (confused)

Aren't they by the hearth, grandfather?

ABEL: I don't see them. (Observing HENRY trying to remove the slippers.) Why, you've got 'em on. Henry.

MRS. SLATER: (promptly) I told him to put them on to stretch them; they were that new and hard. Now, Henry. (MRS. SLATER snatches the slippers from HENRY and gives them ABEL, who puts them on and sits in armchair)

MRS. JORDAN: (to BEN) Well, I don't call that delicate, stepping into a dead man's shoes in such haste.

(*HENRY goes up to the window and pulls up the blind. VICTORIA runs across to ABEL and sits on the floor at his feet.*)

VICTORIA: Oh, Grandpa, I'm so glad you're not dead.

MRS. SLATER: (in a vindictive whisper) Hold your tongue, Victoria.

ABEL: Eh? What's that? Who's gone dead?

MRS. SLATER: (Loudly) Victoria says she's sorry about your head.

ABEL: Ah, thank you, Vicky, but I'm feeling better.

MRS. SLATER (to MRS. JORDAN): He's so fond of Victoria.

MRS. JORDAN (to MRS. SLATER): Yes; he's fond of our Jimmy, too.

MRS. SLATER: You'd better ask him if he promised your Jimmy his gold watch.

MRS. JORDAN: (disconcerted) I couldn't just now. I don't feel equal to it.

ABEL: Why, Ben, you're in mourning! And Lizzie too. And 'Melia, and Henry and little Vicky! Who's gone dead? It's someone in the family. (He chuckles.)

MRS. SLATER: No one you know, father. A relation of Ben's.

ABEL: And what relation of Ben's?

MRS. SLATER: His brother.

BEN (to MRS. SLATER): Hang it, I never had one.

ABEL: Dear, dear. And what was his name, Ben?

BEN: (at a loss) Er - er. (He crosses to front of table.)

MRS. SLATER (R of table, prompting): Frederick.

MRS. JORDAN (L of table, prompting): Albert.

BEN: Er-FedAlb-Issac.

ABEL: Issac? And where did your brother Isaac die?

BEN: In-er-in Australia.

ABEL: Dear, dear. He'd be older than you, eh?

BEN: Yes, five years.

ABEL: Aye, aye. Are you going to the funeral?

BEN: Oh, yes.

MRS. SLATER and MRS. JORDAN: No, no.

BEN: No, of course not.

(He retires to L.)

ABEL: (rising)

Well, I suppose you've only been waiting for me to begin tea. I'm feeling hungry.

MRS. SLATER: (taking up the kettle) I'll make tea.

ABEL: Come along, now; sit you down and let's be jolly.

(*ABEL sits at the head of the table, facing spectators. BEN and MRS. JORDAN on the left. VICTORIA brings a chair and sits by ABEL. MRS. SLATER and HENRY sit on the right. Both the women are next to ABEL.*)

MRS. SLATER: Henry, give grandpa some pie.

ABEL: Thank you. I'll make a start. (He helps himself to bread and butter.)

(HENRY serves the pie and MRS. SLATER pours out tea. Only ABEL eats with any heartiness.)

BEN: Glad to see you've got an appetite, Mr. Merry weather, although you've not been so well.

ABEL: Nothing serious. I've been lying down for a bit.

MRS. SLATER: Been to sleep, grandfather?

ABEL: No, I've not been to sleep.

MRS. SLATER AND HENRY: Oh!

ABEL: (eating and drinking) I can't exactly call everything to mind, but I remember I was a bit dazed, like – I couldn't move an inch, hand or foot.

BEN: And could you see and hear, Mr. Merryweather?

ABEL: Yes, but I don't remember seeing anything particular. Mustard, Ben.

(*BEN passes the mustard.*)

MRS. SLATER: Of course not, grandfather. It was all your fancy. You must have been asleep.

ABEL: (snappishly) I tell you I wasn't asleep, 'Melia. Damnit, I ought to know.

MRS. JORDAN: Didn't you see Henry or Amelia come into the room?

ABEL: (scratching-his head) Now let me think-

MRS. SLATER: I wouldn't press him Elizabeth. Don't press him.

HENRY: I wouldn't worry him.

ABEL: (suddenly recollecting) Ay, begad! 'Melia and Henry, what the devil did you mean by shifting my bureau out of my bedroom? (HENRY and MRS. SLATER are speechless). D' you hear me? Henry! 'Melia!

MRS. JORDAN: What bureau was that. Father?

ABEL: Why, my bureau the one I bought-

MRS. JORDAN: (pointing to the bureau) Was it that one. Father?

ABEL: Ah, that's it. What's it doing here? Eh? (A pause. The clock on the mantelpiece strikes six. Everyone looks at it.)

Drat me if that isn't my clock too. What the devil's been going on in this house? (A slight pause.)

BEN: Well, I'll be hanged.

MRS. JORDAN: I'll tell you what's been going on in this house. Father. Nothing short of robbery.

MRS. SLATER: Be quiet, Elizabeth.

MRS. JORDAN: (rising) I'll not be quiet. Oh, I call it double-faced.

HENRY: Now now, Elizabeth.

MRS. JORDAN: And you, too. Are you such a poor creature that you must do every dirty thing she tells you?

MRS. SLATER: (rising) Remember where you are, Elizabeth.

HENRY: (rising) Come, come. No quarrelling.

BEN: (rising) My wife's every right to speak her own mind.

MRS. SLATER: Then she can speak it outside, not here.

ABEL: (rising: thumping the table) Damn it all, will some one tell me what's been going on?

MRS. JORDAN: Yes, 1 will. I'll not see you robbed.

ABEL: Who's been robbing me?

MRS. JORDAN: Amelia and Henry. They've stolen your clock and bureau. (Working herself up.) They sneaked into your room like a thief in the night and stole them after you were dead.

HENRY AND MRS. SLATER: Hush! Quiet, Elizabeth!

MRS. JORDAN: I'll not be stopped. After you were dead, I say.

ABEL: After who was dead?

MRS. JORDAN: You.

ABEL: But I'm not dead.

MRS. JORDAN: No, but they thought you were. (A pause. ABEL gazes round at them.)

ABEL: Oho! So that's why you're all in black today. You thought I was dead. (He chuckles.) That was a big mistake. (He sits and resumes his tea.)

MRS. SLATER: (sobbing) Grandfather.

ABEL: It didn't take you long to start dividing my things between you.

MRS. JORDAN: No, father; you mustn't think that. Amelia was simply getting hold of them on her own account.

ABEL: You always were a keen one, Amelia. I suppose you thought the will wasn't fair.

HENRY: Did you make a will?

ABEL: Yes, it was locked up in the bureau.

MRS. JORDAN: And what was in it, father?

ABEL: That doesn't matter now. I'm thinking of destroying it and making another.

MRS. SLATER: (sobbing) Grandfather, you'll not be hard on me.

ABEL: I'll trouble you for another cup of tea, 'Melia; two lumps and plenty of milk.

MRS. SLATER: With pleasure. Grandfather. (She pours out the tea.)

ABEL: I don't want to be hard on anyone. I'll tell you what I'm going to do. Since your mother died, I've lived part of the time with you, 'Melia, and part with you, Lizzie. Well, I shall make a new will, leaving all my bits of things to whomever I'm living with when I die. How does that strike you?

HENRY: It's a bit of a lottery-like.

MRS. JORDAN: And who do you intend to live with from now?

ABEL: (drinking his tea) I'm just coming to that.

MRS. JORDAN: You know, father, it's quite time you came to live with us again. We'd make you very comfortable.

MRS. SLATER: No, he's not been with us as long as he was with you.

MRS. JORDAN: I may be wrong, but I don't think father will fancy living on with you after what's happened today.

ABEL: So you'd like to have me again, Lizzie?

MRS. JORDAN: You know we're ready for you to make your home with us for as long you please.

ABEL: What do you say to that, 'Melia?

MRS. SLATER: All I can say is that Elizabeth's changed her mind in the last two years. (Rising). Grandfather, do you know what the quarrel between us was about?

MRS. JORDAN: Amelia, don't be a fool; sit down.

MRS. SLATER: No, if I'm not to have him, you shan't either. We quarrelled because Elizabeth said she wouldn't take you off our hands at any price. She said she'd enough of you to last a lifetime, and we'd got to keep you.

ABEL: It seems to me that neither of you has any cause to feel proud about the way you've treated me.

MRS. SLATER: If I've done anything wrong. I'm sure I'm sorry for it.

MRS. JORDAN: And I can't say more than that, too.

ABEL: It's a bit late to say it, now. You neither of you cared to put up with me.

MRS. SLATER AND MRS. JORDAN: No, no grandfather.

ABEL: Aye, you both say that because of what I've told you about leaving my money. Well, since you don't want me I'll go to someone that does.

BEN: Come Mr. Merryweather, you've got to live with one of your daughters.

ABEL: I'll tell you what I've got to do. On Monday next I've got to do three things. I've got to go to the lawyer's and alter my will; and I've got to go to the insurance office and pay my premium; and I've got to go to St. Philip's Church and get married.

BEN AND HENRY: What!

MRS. JORDAN: Get married!

MRS. SLATER: He's out of his senses. (General consternation.)

ABEL: I say I'm going to get married.

MRS. SLATER: Who to?

ABEL: To Mrs. John Shorrocks who keeps the 'Ring-o' -Bells. We've had it fixed up a good while now, but I was keeping it for a pleasant surprise. (He rises.) I felt I was a bit of a burden to you, so I found someone who'd think it a pleasure to look after me. We shall be very glad to see you at the ceremony. (He gets to the door.) Till Monday, then. Twelve o' clock at St. Philip's Church. (Opening the door.) It's a good thing you brought that bureau downstairs, 'Melia. It'll be handier to carry across to the 'Ring-o' -Bells on Monday. (He goes out.)

The curtain falls.

Exercise

I. Expansion of Idea

1. Greed leads to loss.
2. Family bonds are more valuable than wealth.
3. Hypocrisy destroys respect.
4. Appearances can be deceptive.
5. Timely action prevents misunderstandings.

Sample Expansion:

Greed leads to loss.

Greed is a dangerous human trait that often results in loss and regret. In Stanley Houghton's *The Dear Departed*, Mrs. Slater and Mrs. Jordan's greed for their father Abel Merryweather's possessions leads to quarrels, dishonesty, and humiliation. Even before confirming his death, they begin dividing his belongings, showing how material desires can destroy family bonds. However, their greed turns into shame when Abel, very much alive, decides to leave them and marry someone else. This incident teaches that greed never brings true happiness; instead, it causes people to lose what really matters — love, respect, and relationships. Similarly, in real life, people who prioritize wealth over values often end up lonely and dissatisfied. Therefore, one must control selfish desires and value people more than possessions.

II. The main incidents in the play are in a jumbled order. Arrange them in the sequence in which they occur in the play:

1. The family sits down to have tea.
2. The Slaters fetch the bureau and the clock from upstairs
3. Mrs. Slater discovers that grandfather is 'dead'.
4. Grandfather announces his intension to change his will and to marry Mrs. Shorrocks
5. Grandfather comes down and is surprised to find the Jordans.
6. The Jordans arrive and learn the details of grandfather's demise.

7. Grandfather comes to know how his daughters were in a hurry to divide his things between them.

III. Discuss in groups about the problems faced by the elderly people in our society and write in a paragraph or two.

The Gift of the Magi

O' Henry

ONE DOLLAR AND EIGHTY-SEVEN CENTS. That was all. She had put it aside, one cent and then another and then another, in her careful buying of meat and other food. Della counted it three times. One dollar and eighty-seven cents. And the next day would be **Christmas**.

There was nothing to do but fall on the bed and cry. So Della did it.

While the lady of the home is slowly growing quieter, we can look at the home. **Furnished** rooms at a cost of $8 a week. There is little more to say about it.

In the hall below was a letter-box too small to hold a letter. There was an electric bell, but it could not make a sound. Also there was a name beside the door: "Mr. James Dillingham Young."

When the name was placed there, Mr. James Dillingham Young was being paid $30 a week. Now, when he was being paid only $20 a week, the name seemed too long and important. It should perhaps have been "Mr. James D. Young." But when Mr. James Dillingham Young entered the furnished rooms, his name became very short indeed. Mrs. James Dillingham Young put her arms warmly about him and called him "Jim." You have already met her. She is Della.

Della finished her crying and cleaned the marks of it from her face. She stood by the window and looked out with no interest. Tomorrow would be Christmas Day, and she had only $1.87 with which to buy Jim a gift. She had put aside as much as she could for months, with this result. Twenty dollars a week is not much. Everything had cost more than she had expected. It always happened like that.

Only $ 1.87 to buy a gift for Jim. Her Jim. She had had many happy hours planning something nice for him. Something nearly good enough. Something almost worth the honor of belonging to Jim.

There was a looking-glass between the windows of the room. Perhaps you have seen the kind of looking-glass that is placed in $8 furnished rooms. It was very narrow. A person could see only a little of himself at a time. However, if he was very thin and moved very quickly, he might be able to get a good view of himself. Della, being quite thin, had mastered this art.

Suddenly she turned from the window and stood before the glass. Her eyes were shining brightly, but her face had lost its color. Quickly she pulled down her hair and let it fall to its complete length.

The James Dillingham Youngs were very proud of two things which they owned. One thing was Jim's gold watch. It had once belonged to his father. And, long ago, it had belonged to his father's father. The other thing was Della's hair.

If a queen had lived in the rooms near theirs, Della would have washed and dried her hair where the queen could see it. Della knew her hair was more beautiful than any queen's jewels and gifts.

If a king had lived in the same house, with all his riches, Jim would have looked at his watch every time they met. Jim knew that no king had anything so valuable.

So now Della's beautiful hair fell about her, shining like a falling stream of brown water. It reached below her knee. It almost made itself into a dress for her.

And then she put it up on her head again, nervously and quickly. Once she stopped for a moment and stood still while a tear or two ran down her face.

She put on her old brown coat. She put on her old brown hat. With the bright light still in her eyes, she moved quickly out the door and down to the street.

Where she stopped, the sign said: “Mrs. Sofronie. Hair Articles of all Kinds.”

Up to the second floor Della ran, and stopped to get her breath.

Mrs. Sofronie, large, too white, cold-eyed, looked at her.

“Will you buy my hair?” asked Della.

“I buy hair,” said Mrs. Sofronie. “Take your hat off and let me look at it.”

Down fell the brown waterfall.

“Twenty dollars,” said Mrs. Sofronie, lifting the hair to feel its weight.

“Give it to me quick,” said Della.

Oh, and the next two hours seemed to fly. She was going from one shop to another, to find a gift for Jim.

She found it at last. It surely had been made for Jim and no one else. There was no other like it in any of the shops, and she had looked in every shop in the city.

It was a gold watch chain, very simply made. Its value was in its rich and pure material. Because it was so plain and simple, you knew that it was very valuable. All good things are like this.

It was good enough for The Watch.

As soon as she saw it, she knew that Jim must have it. It was like him. Quietness and value—Jim and the chain both had quietness and value. She paid twenty-one dollars for it. And she hurried home with the chain and eighty-seven cents.

With that chain on his watch, Jim could look at his watch and learn the time anywhere he might be. Though the watch was so fine, it had never had a fine chain. He sometimes took it out and looked at it only when no one could see him do it.

When Della arrived home, her mind quieted a little. She began to think more reasonably. She started to try to cover the sad marks of what she had done. Love and large-hearted giving, when added together, can leave deep marks. It is never easy to cover these marks, dear friends—never easy.

Within forty minutes her head looked a little better. With her short hair, she looked wonderfully like a schoolboy. She stood at the looking-glass for a long time.

"If Jim doesn't kill me," she said to herself, "before he looks at me a second time, he'll say I look like a girl who sings and dances for money. But what could I do—oh! What could I do with a dollar and eighty-seven cents?"

At seven, Jim's dinner was ready for him.

Jim was never late. Della held the watch chain in her hand and sat near the door where he always entered. Then she heard his step in the hall and her face lost color for a moment. She often said little prayers quietly, about simple everyday things. And now she said: "Please God, make him think I'm still pretty."

The door opened and Jim stepped in. He looked very thin and he was not smiling. Poor fellow, he was only twenty-two—and with a family to take care of! He needed a new coat and he had nothing to cover his cold hands.

Jim stopped inside the door. He was as quiet as a hunting dog when it is near a bird. His eyes looked strangely at Della, and there was an expression in them that she could not understand. It filled her with fear. It was not anger, nor surprise, nor anything she had been ready for. He simply looked at her with that strange expression on his face.

Della went to him.

"Jim, dear," she cried, "don't look at me like that. I had my hair cut off and sold it. I couldn't live through Christmas without giving you a

gift. My hair will grow again. You won't care, will you? My hair grows very fast. It's Christmas, Jim. Let's be happy. You don't know what a nice—what a beautiful nice gift I got for you."

"You've cut off your hair?" asked Jim slowly. He seemed to labor to understand what had happened. He seemed not to feel sure he knew.

"Cut it off and sold it," said Della. "Don't you like me now? I'm me, Jim. I'm the same without my hair."

Jim looked around the room.

"You say your hair is gone?" he said.

"You don't have to look for it," said Della. "It's sold, I tell you—sold and gone, too. It's the night before Christmas, boy. Be good to me, because I sold it for you. Maybe the hairs of my head could be counted," she said, "but no one could ever count my love for you. Shall we eat dinner, Jim?"

Jim put his arms around his Della. For ten seconds let us look in another direction. Eight dollars a week or a million dollars a year—how different are they? Someone may give you an answer, but it will be wrong. The **magi** brought valuable gifts, but that was not among them. My meaning will be explained soon.

From inside the coat, Jim took something tied in paper. He threw it upon the table.

"I want you to understand me, Dell," he said. "Nothing like a haircut could make me love you any less. But if you'll open that, you may know what I felt when I came in."

White fingers pulled off the paper. And then a cry of joy; and then a change to tears.

For there lay The **Combs**—the combs that Della had seen in a shop window and loved for a long time. Beautiful combs, with jewels, perfect for her beautiful hair. She had known they cost too much for her to buy them. She had looked at them without the least hope of owning them. And now they were hers, but her hair was gone.

But she held them to her heart, and at last was able to look up and say: "My hair grows so fast, Jim!"

And then she jumped up and cried, "Oh, oh!"

Jim had not yet seen his beautiful gift. She held it out to him in her open hand. The gold seemed to shine softly as if with her own warm and loving spirit.

"Isn't it perfect, Jim? I hunted all over town to find it. You'll have to look at your watch a hundred times a day now. Give me your watch. I want to see how they look together."

Jim sat down and smiled.

"Della," said he, "let's put our Christmas gifts away and keep them a while. They're too nice to use now. I sold the watch to get the money to buy the combs. And now I think we should have our dinner."

The magi, as you know, were wise men—wonderfully wise men— who brought gifts to the newborn Christ-child. They were the first to give Christmas gifts. Being wise, their gifts were doubtless wise ones. And here I have told you the story of two children who were not wise. Each sold the most valuable thing he owned in order to buy a gift for the other. But let me speak a last word to the wise of these days: Of all who give gifts, these two were the most wise. Of all who give and receive gifts, such as they are the most wise. Everywhere they are the wise ones. They are the magi.

Exercise

The Gift of the Magi by O. Henry is a touching short story about a young couple, Jim and Della, who are poor but deeply in love. Della sells her beautiful, long hair to buy a chain for Jim's watch, as a Christmas gift. Meanwhile, Jim sells his watch to buy combs for Della's hair. Both gifts turn out to be unusable, but they realize their greatest gift is their selfless love for each other. The story conveys the values of sacrifice, love, and true generosity.

I. Write a Newspaper Ad

Compose a newspaper advertisement from Jim's perspective, his decision to sell his watch. Include details about the watch and its sentimental value.

II. Modern Adaptation

Rewrite the story in a contemporary setting, considering how Jim and Della's sacrifices would manifest today. For example, would they sell their smartphones?

III. Debate the Ethics

Write your opinion on whether Jim and Della made wise decisions in selling their prized possessions. Use evidence from the text to support arguments.

On the Love of Life

William Hazlitt

It is our intention, in the course of these papers, occasionally to expose certain vulgar errors, which have crept into our reasonings on men and manners. Perhaps one of the most interesting of these, is that which relates to the source of our general attachment to life. We are not going to enter into the question, whether life is, on the whole, to be regarded as a blessing, though we are by no means inclined to adopt the opinion of that sage, who thought "that the best thing that could have happened to a man was never to have been born, and the next best to have died the moment after he came into existence." The common argument, however, which is made use of to prove the value of life, from the strong desire which almost everyone feels for its continuance, appears to be altogether inconclusive. The wise and the foolish, the weak and the strong, the lame and the blind, the prisoner and the free, the prosperous and the wretched, the beggar and the king, the rich and the poor, the young and the old, from the little child who tries to leap over his own shadow, to the old man who stumbles blindfold on his grave, all feel this desire in common. Our notions with respect to the importance of life, and our attachment to it, depend on a principle which has very little to do with its happiness or its misery.

The love of life is, in general, the effect not of our enjoyments, but of our passions. We are not attached to it so much for its own sake, or as it is connected with happiness, as because it is necessary to action. Without life there can be no action – no objects of pursuit – no restless desires – no tormenting passions. Hence it is that we fondly cling to it – that we dread its termination as the close, not of enjoyment, but of hope. The proof that our attachment to life is not absolutely owing to the immediate satisfaction we find in it, is, that those persons are commonly found most loath to part with it who have the least enjoyment of it, and who have the greatest difficulties to struggle with, as losing gamesters are the most desperate. And farther, there are not many persons who, with all their pretended love of life, would not, if it had been in their power, have melted down the longest life to a few hours. "The school-boy, " says Addison, "counts the time till the return of the holidays; the minor longs to be of age; the lover is impatient till he is married." – "Hope and fantastic expectations spend much of our lives; and while with passion we look for a coronation, or the death of an enemy, or a day of joy, passing from fancy to possession without any intermediate notices, we throw away a precious year." JEREMY TAYLOR. – We would willingly, and without remorse, sacrifice the present moment, but all the interval (no matter how long) that separates us from any favourite object. We chiefly look upon life, then, as the means to an end. Its common enjoyments and its daily evils are alike disregarded for any idle purpose we have in view. It should seem as if there were a few green sunny spots in the desert of life, to which we are always hastening forward: we eye them wistfully in the distance, and care not what perils or suffering we endure, so that we arrive at them at last. However, weary we may be of the same stale round – however sick of the past – however hopeless of the future – the mind still revolts at the thought of death, because the fancied possibility of good, which always remains with life, gathers strength as it is about to be torn from us for forever, and the dullest scene looks bright compared with the darkness of the grave. Our reluctance to part with existence evidently does not depend on the calm and even current of our lives, but on the force and impulse of the passions. Hence that indifference to death which has been sometimes remarked in people who lead a solitary and peaceful life in remote and barren districts. The pulse of life in them does not beat strong enough to occasion any violent revulsion of the frame when it ceases. He who treads the green mountain turf, or who sleeps beneath it, enjoys and almost equal quiet. The death of those persons has always been accounted happy, who had attained their utmost wishes, who had nothing left to regret or to desire. Our repugnance to death increases in proportion to our consciousness of having lived in vain – to the violence of our efforts and the keenness of our disappointments – and to our earnest desire to find in the future, if possible a rich amends for the past. We may be said to nurse our existence with the greatest tenderness, according to the pain it has cost us; and feel at every step of our varying progress the truth of that line of the poet – "An ounce of sweet is worth a pound of sour."

The love of life is in fact the sum of all our passions and of all our enjoyments; but these are by no means the same thing, for the vehemence of our passions is irritated, not less by disappointment than by the prospect of success. Nothing seems to be a match for this general tenaciousness of existence, but such an extremity either of bodily or mental suffering as destroys at once the power both of habit and imagination. In short, the question whether life is accompanied with a greater quantity of pleasure or pain, may be fairly set aside as frivolous, and of no practical utility; for our attachment to life depends on our interest in it; and it cannot be denied that we have more interest in this moving, busy scene, agitated with a thousand hopes and fears, and checkered with every diversity of joy and sorrow, than in a dreary blank. To be something is better than to be nothing, because we can feel no interest in nothing. Passion, imagination, self-will, the sense of power, the very consciousness of our existence, bind us to life, and hold us fast in its chains, as by a magic spell, in spite of every other consideration. Nothing can be more philosophical than the reasoning which Milton puts into the mouth of the fallen angel:

— "And that must end us, that must be our cure,
To be no more; sad cure: for who would lose,
Though full of pain, this intellectual being,

Those thoughts that wander through eternity,
To perish rather, swallow'd up and lost
In the wide womb of uncreated night,
Devoid of sense and motion?"

Nearly the same account may be given in answer to the question which has been asked, Why so few tyrants kill themselves? In the first place, they are never satisfied with the mischief they have done, and cannot quit their hold of power, after all sense of pleasure is fled. Besides, they absurdly argue from the means of happiness placed within their reach to the end itself; and, dazzled by the pomp and pageantry of a throne, cannot relinquish the persuasion that they ought to be happier than other men. The prejudice of opinion, which attaches us to life, is in them stronger than in others, and incorrigible to experience. The Great are life's fools -- dupes of the splendid shadows that surround them, and wedded to the very mockeries of opinion.

Whatever is our situation or pursuit in life, the result will be much the same. The strength of the passion seldom corresponds to the pleasure we find in its indulgence. The miser "robs himself to increase his store"; the ambitious man toils up a slippery precipice only to be tumbled headlong from its height; the lover is infatuated with the charms of his mistress, exactly in proportion to the mortifications he has received from her. Even those who succeed in nothing, who, as it has been emphatically expressed –

— "Are made desperate by too quick a sense
Of constant infelicity; cut off
From peace like exiles, on some barren rock,
Their life's sad prison, with no more of ease,
Than sentinels between two armies set;"

are yet as unwilling as others to give over the unprofitable strife: their harassed feverish existence refuses rest, and frets the languor of exhausted hope into the torture of unavailing regret. The exile, who has been unexpectedly restored to his country and to liberty, often finds his courage fail with the accomplishment of all his wishes, and the struggle of life and hope ceases at the same instant.

We once more repeat, that we do not, in the forgoing remarks mean to enter into a comparative estimate of the value of human life, but merely to shew, that the strength of our attachment to it is a very fallacious test of its happiness.

Exercise

In *On the Love of Life*, William Hazlitt reflects on the deep human desire to keep living, even during suffering or hardship. He argues that life is valuable not just because of pleasure or success, but because of the simple experience of being alive. Hazlitt admires the strength of the human spirit and how people cling to life with hope, even when things seem hopeless. The essay celebrates life itself as something worth holding on to.

Podcasts

A podcast is essentially a digital audio or video show, similar to a radio program, that you can listen to or watch on demand. It's a series of audio or video files (episodes) that are available for download or streaming over the internet.

Features:

1. Podcasts are typically released in episodes, with new content added regularly.
2. Listeners can access episodes at any time, unlike traditional radio or TV.
3. Podcasts cover a wide range of subjects, from news and education to entertainment and storytelling.

Formats:

1. Interviews
2. Storytelling
3. Panel discussions
4. Solo shows

I. Structure and plan a podcast episode on a topic you're passionate about.

II. Write a day's Journal of self-reflection.

III. Write a few self-affirmation Phrases that will boost confidence.

Nobel Prize Acceptance Speech

Wangari Maathai

Your Majesties
Your Royal Highnesses
Honourable Members of the Norwegian Nobel Committee
Excellencies, Ladies and Gentlemen

I stand before you and the world humbled by this recognition and uplifted by the honour of being the 2004 Nobel Peace Laureate.

As the first African woman to receive this prize, I accept it on behalf of the people of Kenya and Africa, and indeed the world. I am especially mindful of women and the girl child. I hope it will encourage them to raise their voices and take more space for leadership. I know the honour also gives a deep sense of pride to our men, both old and young. As a mother, I appreciate the inspiration this brings to the youth and urge them to use it to pursue their dreams.

Although this prize comes to me, it acknowledges the work of countless individuals and groups across the globe. They work quietly and often without recognition to protect the environment, promote democracy, defend human rights and ensure equality between women and men. By so doing, they plant seeds of peace. I know they, too, are proud today. To all who feel represented by this prize I say use it to advance your mission and meet the high expectations the world will place on us.

This honour is also for my family, friends, partners and supporters throughout the world. All of them helped shape the vision and sustain our work, which was often accomplished under hostile conditions. I am also grateful to the people of Kenya – who remained stubbornly hopeful that democracy could be realized and their environment managed sustainably. Because of this support, I am here today to accept this great honour.

I am immensely privileged to join my fellow African Peace laureates, Presidents Nelson Mandela and F.W. de Klerk, Archbishop Desmond Tutu, the late Chief Albert Luthuli, the late Anwar el-Sadat and the UN Secretary General, Kofi Annan.

I know that African people everywhere are encouraged by this news. My fellow Africans, as we embrace this recognition, let us use it to intensify our commitment to our people, to reduce conflicts and poverty and thereby improve their quality of life. Let us embrace democratic governance, protect human rights and protect our environment. I am confident that we shall rise to the occasion. I have always believed that solutions to most of our problems must come from us.

In this year's prize, the Norwegian Nobel Committee has placed the critical issue of environment and its linkage to democracy and peace before the world. For their visionary action, I am profoundly grateful. Recognizing that sustainable development, democracy and peace are indivisible is an idea whose time has come. Our work over the past 30 years has always appreciated and engaged these linkages.

My inspiration partly comes from my childhood experiences and observations of Nature in rural Kenya. It has been influenced and nurtured by the formal education I was privileged to receive in Kenya, the United States and Germany. As I was growing up, I witnessed forests being cleared and replaced by commercial plantations, which destroyed local biodiversity and the capacity of the forests to conserve water.

Excellencies, ladies and gentlemen,

In 1977, when we started the Green Belt Movement, I was partly responding to needs identified by rural women, namely lack of firewood, clean drinking water, balanced diets, shelter and income.

Throughout Africa, women are the primary caretakers, holding significant responsibility for tilling the land and feeding their families. As a result, they are often the first to become aware of environmental damage as resources become scarce and incapable of sustaining their families.

The women we worked with recounted that unlike in the past, they were unable to meet their basic needs. This was due to the degradation of their immediate environment as well as the introduction of commercial farming, which replaced the growing of household food crops. But international trade controlled the price of the exports from these small-scale farmers and a reasonable and just income could not be guaranteed. I came to understand that when the environment is destroyed, plundered or mismanaged, we undermine our quality of life and that of future generations.

Tree planting became a natural choice to address some of the initial basic needs identified by women. Also, tree planting is simple, attainable and guarantees quick, successful results within a reasonable amount time. This sustains interest and commitment.

So, together, we have planted over 30 million trees that provide fuel, food, shelter, and income to support their children's education and household needs. The activity also creates employment and improves soils and watersheds. Through their involvement, women gain some degree of power over their lives, especially their social and economic position and relevance in the family. This work continues.

Initially, the work was difficult because historically our people have been persuaded to believe that because they are poor, they lack not only capital, but also knowledge and skills to address their challenges. Instead, they are conditioned to believe that solutions to their problems must come from 'outside'. Further, women did not realize that meeting their needs depended on their environment being healthy and well managed. They were also unaware that a degraded environment leads to a scramble for scarce resources and may culminate in poverty and even conflict. They were also unaware of the injustices of international economic arrangements.

In order to assist communities to understand these linkages, we developed a citizen education program, during which people identify their problems, the causes and possible solutions. They then make connections between their own personal actions and the problems they witness in the environment and in society. They learn that our world is confronted with a litany of woes: corruption, violence against women and children, disruption and breakdown of families, and disintegration of cultures and communities. They also identify the abuse of drugs and chemical substances, especially among young people. There are also devastating diseases that are defying cures or occurring in epidemic proportions. Of particular concern are HIV/AIDS, malaria and diseases associated with malnutrition.

On the environment front, they are exposed to many human activities that are devastating to the environment and societies. These include widespread destruction of ecosystems, especially through deforestation, climatic instability, and contamination in the soils and waters that all contribute to excruciating poverty.

In the process, the participants discover that they must be part of the solutions. They realize their hidden potential and are empowered to overcome inertia and take action. They come to recognize that they are the primary custodians and beneficiaries of the environment that sustains them.

Entire communities also come to understand that while it is necessary to hold their governments accountable, it is equally important that in their own relationships with each other, they exemplify the leadership values they wish to see in their own leaders, namely justice, integrity and trust.

Although initially the Green Belt Movement's tree planting activities did not address issues of democracy and peace, it soon became clear that responsible governance of the environment was impossible without democratic space. Therefore, the tree became a symbol for the democratic struggle in Kenya. Citizens were mobilised to challenge widespread abuses of power, corruption and environmental mismanagement. In Nairobi 's Uhuru Park, at Freedom Corner, and in many parts of the country, trees of peace were planted to demand the release of prisoners of conscience and a peaceful transition to democracy.

Through the Green Belt Movement, thousands of ordinary citizens were mobilized and empowered to take action and effect change. They learned to overcome fear and a sense of helplessness and moved to defend democratic rights.

In time, the tree also became a symbol for peace and conflict resolution, especially during ethnic conflicts in Kenya when the Green Belt Movement used peace trees to reconcile disputing communities. During the ongoing re-writing of the Kenyan constitution, similar trees of peace were planted in many parts of the country to promote a culture of peace. Using trees as a symbol of peace is in keeping with a widespread African tradition. For example, the elders of the Kikuyu carried a staff from the *thigi* tree that, when placed between two disputing sides, caused them to stop fighting and seek reconciliation. Many communities in Africa have these traditions.

Such practices are part of an extensive cultural heritage, which contributes both to the conservation of habitats and to cultures of peace. With the destruction of these cultures and the introduction of new values, local biodiversity is no longer valued or protected and as a result, it is quickly degraded and disappears. For this reason, The Green Belt Movement explores the concept of cultural biodiversity, especially with respect to indigenous seeds and medicinal plants.

As we progressively understood the causes of environmental degradation, we saw the need for good governance. Indeed, the state of any county's environment is a reflection of the kind of governance in place, and without good governance there can be no peace. Many countries, which have poor governance systems, are also likely to have conflicts and poor laws protecting the environment.

In 2002, the courage, resilience, patience and commitment of members of the Green Belt Movement, other civil society organizations, and the Kenyan public culminated in the peaceful transition to a democratic government and laid the foundation for a more stable society.

Excellencies, friends, ladies and gentlemen,

It is 30 years since we started this work. Activities that devastate the environment and societies continue unabated. Today we are faced with a challenge that calls for a shift in our thinking, so that humanity stops threatening its life-support system. We are called to assist the Earth to heal her wounds and, in the process, heal our own – indeed, to embrace the whole creation in all its diversity, beauty and wonder. This will happen if we see the need to revive our sense of belonging to a larger family of life, with which we have shared our evolutionary process.

In the course of history, there comes a time when humanity is called to shift to a new level of consciousness, to reach a higher moral ground. A time when we have to shed our fear and give hope to each other.

That time is now.

The Norwegian Nobel Committee has challenged the world to broaden the understanding of peace: there can be no peace without equitable development; and there can be no development without sustainable management of the environment in a democratic and peaceful space. This shift is an idea whose time has come.

I call on leaders, especially from Africa, to expand democratic space and build fair and just societies that allow the creativity and energy of their citizens to flourish. Those of us who have been privileged to receive education, skills, and experiences and even power must be role models for the next generation of leadership. In this regard, I would also like to appeal for the freedom of my fellow laureate Aung San Suu Kyi so that she can continue her work for peace and democracy for the people of Burma and the world at large.

Culture plays a central role in the political, economic and social life of communities. Indeed, culture may be the missing link in the development of Africa. Culture is dynamic and evolves over time, consciously discarding retrogressive traditions, like female genital mutilation (FGM), and embracing aspects that are good and useful.

Africans, especially, should re-discover positive aspects of their culture. In accepting them, they would give themselves a sense of belonging, identity and self-confidence.

Ladies and Gentlemen,

There is also need to galvanize civil society and grassroots movements to catalyse change. I call upon governments to recognize the role of these social movements in building a critical mass of responsible citizens, who help maintain checks and balances in society. On their part, civil society should embrace not only their rights but also their responsibilities.

Further, industry and global institutions must appreciate that ensuring economic justice, equity and ecological integrity are of greater value than profits at any cost. The extreme global inequities and prevailing consumption patterns continue at the expense of the environment and peaceful co-existence. The choice is ours.

I would like to call on young people to commit themselves to activities that contribute toward achieving their long-term dreams. They have the energy and creativity to shape a sustainable future. To the young people I say, you are a gift to your communities and indeed the world. You are our hope and our future.

The holistic approach to development, as exemplified by the Green Belt Movement, could be embraced and replicated in more parts of Africa and beyond. It is for this reason that I have established the Wangari Maathai Foundation to ensure the continuation and expansion of these activities. Although a lot has been achieved, much remains to be done.

Excellencies, ladies and gentlemen,

As I conclude I reflect on my childhood experience when I would visit a stream next to our home to fetch water for my mother. I would drink water straight from the stream. Playing among the arrowroot leaves I tried in vain to pick up the strands of frogs' eggs, believing they were beads. But every time I put my little fingers under them, they would break. Later, I saw thousands of tadpoles: black, energetic and wriggling through the clear water against the background of the brown earth. This is the world I inherited from my parents.

Today, over 50 years later, the stream has dried up, women walk long distances for water, which is not always clean, and children will never know what they have lost. The challenge is to restore the home of the tadpoles and give back to our children a world of beauty and wonder.

Thank you very much.

Exercise

I. Find out the Honorifics mentioned in the Nobel Lecture by Wangari Maathai:

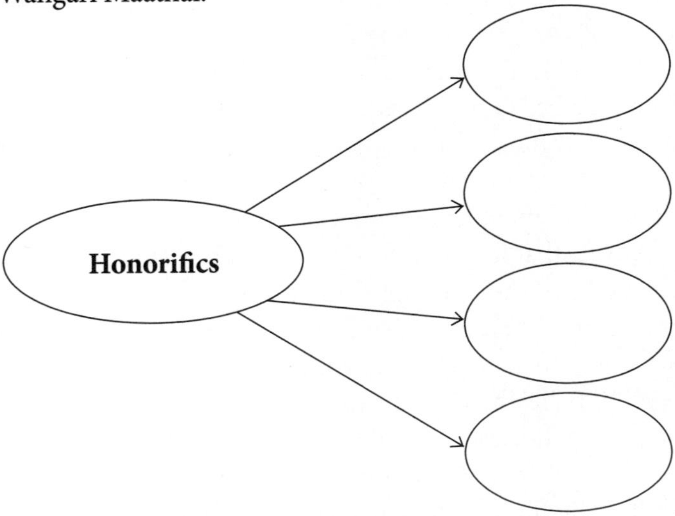

II. Maathai's Green Belt Movement led to the planting of over 30 million trees in Kenya creating Economic conservation. Design a Poster to conserve the nature in your neighbourhood.

III. Write a few slogans for the promotion of Women's Rights.

Of Friendship

Francis Bacon

It had been hard for him that spake it to have put more truth and untruth together in few words, than in that speech. Whatsoever is delighted in solitude, is either a wild beast or a god. For it is most true, that a natural and secret hatred, and aversation towards society, in any man, hath somewhat of the savage beast; but it is most untrue, that it should have any character at all, of the divine nature; except it proceed, not out of a pleasure in solitude, but out of a love and desire to sequester a man's self, for a higher conversation: such as is found to have been falsely and feignedly in some of the heathen; as Epimenides the Candian, Numa the Roman, Empedocles the Sicilian, and Apollonius of Tyana; and truly and really, in divers of the ancient hermits and holy fathers of the church. But little do men perceive what solitude is, and how far it extendeth. For a crowd is not company; and faces are but a gallery of pictures; and talk but a tinkling cymbal, where there is no love. The Latin adage meeteth with it a little: Magna civitas, magna solitudo; because in a great town friends are scattered; so that there is not that fellowship, for the most part, which is in less neighborhoods. But we may go further, and affirm most truly, that it is a mere and miserable solitude to want true friends; without which the world is but a wilderness; and even in this sense also of solitude, whosoever in the frame of his nature and affections, is unfit for friendship, he taketh it of the beast, and not from humanity. A principal fruit of friendship, is the ease and discharge of the fulness and swellings of the heart, which passions of all kinds do cause and induce. We know diseases of stoppings, and suffocations, are the most dangerous in the body; and it is not much otherwise in the mind; you may take sarza to open the liver, steel to open the spleen, flowers of sulphur for the lungs, castoreum for the brain; but no receipt openeth the heart, but a true friend; to whom you may impart griefs, joys, fears, hopes, suspicions, counsels, and whatsoever lieth upon the heart to oppress it, in a kind of civil shrift or confession. It is a strange thing to observe, how high a rate great kings and monarchs do set upon this fruit of friendship, whereof we speak: so great, as they purchase it, many times, at the hazard of their own safety and greatness. For princes, in regard of the distance of their fortune from that of their subjects and servants, cannot gather this fruit, except (to make themselves capable there of) they raise some persons to be, as it were, companions and almost equals to themselves, which many times sorteth to inconvenience. The modern languages give unto such persons the name of favorites, or privadoes; as if it were matter of grace, or conversation. But the Roman name attaineth the true use and cause thereof, naming them participes curarum; for it is that which tieth the knot. And we see plainly that this hath been done, not by weak and passionate princes only, but by the wisest and most politic that ever reigned; who have oftentimes joined to themselves some of their servants; whom both themselves have called friends, and allowed other likewise to call them in the same manner; using the word which is received between private men. L. Sylla, when he commanded Rome, raised Pompey (after surnamed the Great) to that height, that Pompey vaunted himself for Sylla's overmatch. For when he had carried the consulship for a friend of his, against the pursuit of Sylla, and that Sylla did a little resent thereat, and began to speak great, Pompey turned upon him again, and in effect bade him be quiet; for that more men adored the sun rising, than the sun setting. With Julius Caesar, Decimus Brutus had obtained that interest, as he set him down, in his testament, for heir in remainder, after his nephew. And this was the man that had power with him, to draw him forth to his death. For when Caesar would have discharged the senate, in regard of some ill presages, and specially a dream of Calpurnia; this man lifted him gently by the arm out of his chair, telling him he hoped he would not dismiss the senate, till his wife had dreamt a better dream. And it seemeth his favor was so great, as Antonius, in a letter which is recited verbatim in one of Cicero's Philippics, calleth him venefica, witch; as if he had enchanted Caesar. Augustus raised Agrippa (though of mean birth) to that height, as when he consulted with Maecenas, about the marriage of his daughter Julia, Maecenas took the liberty to tell him, that he must either marry his daughter to Agrippa, or take away his life; there was no third war, he had made him so great. With Tiberius Caesar, Sejanus had ascended to that height, as they two were termed, and reckoned, as a pair of friends. Tiberius in a letter to him saith, Haec pro amicitia nostra non occultavi; and the whole senate dedicated an altar to Friendship, as to a goddess, in respect of the great dearness of friendship, between them two. The like, or more, was between Septimius Severus and Plautianus. For he forced his eldest son to marry the daughter of Plautianus; and would often maintain Plautianus, in doing affronts to his son; and did write also in a letter to the senate, by these words: I love the man so well, as I wish he may over-live me. Now if these princes had been as a Trajan, or a Marcus Aurelius, a man might have thought that this had proceeded of an abundant goodness of nature; but being men so wise, of such strength and severity of mind, and so extreme lovers of themselves, as all these were, it proveth most plainly that they found their own felicity (though as great as ever happened to mortal men) but as an half piece, except they mought have a friend, to make it entire; and yet, which is more, they were princes that had wives, sons, nephews; and yet all these could not supply the comfort of friendship. It is not to be forgotten, what Comineus observeth of his first master, Duke Charles the Hardy, namely, that he would communicate his secrets with none; and least of all, those secrets which troubled him most. Whereupon he goeth on, and saith that towards his latter time, that closeness did impair, and a little perish his understanding. Surely Comineus mought have made the same judgment also, if it had pleased him, of his second master, Lewis the Eleventh, whose closeness was indeed his tormentor. The parable of Pythagoras is dark, but true; Cor ne edito; Eat not the heart. Certainly if a man would give it a hard phrase, those that want friends, to open themselves unto are cannibals of their own hearts. But one thing is most admirable (wherewith I will conclude this first fruit of friendship), which is, that this communicating of a man's self to his friend, works two contrary effects; for it redoubleth joys, and cutteth griefs in halves. For there is no man, that imparteth his joys to his friend, but he joyeth the more; and no man that imparteth his griefs to his friend, but he grieveth the less. So that it is in truth, of operation upon a man's mind, of like virtue as the alchemists use to attribute to their stone, for man's body; that it worketh all contrary effects, but still to the good and benefit of nature. But yet without praying in aid of alchemists, there is a manifest image of this, in the ordinary course of nature. For in bodies, union strengtheneth and cherisheth any natural action; and on the other side, weakeneth and dulleth any violent impression: and even so it is of minds. The second fruit of friendship, is healthful and sovereign for the understanding, as the first is for the affections. For friendship maketh indeed a fair day in the affections, from storm and tempests; but it maketh daylight in the understanding, out of darkness, and confusion of thoughts. Neither is this to be understood only of faithful counsel, which a man receiveth from his friend; but before you come to that, certain it is, that whosoever hath his mind fraught with many thoughts, his wits and understanding do clarify and break up, in the communicating and discoursing with another; he tosseth his thoughts more easily; he marshalleth them more orderly, he seeth how they look when they are turned into words: finally, he waxeth wiser than himself; and that more by an hour's discourse, than by a day's meditation. It was well said by Themistocles, to the king of Persia, That speech was like cloth of Arras, opened and put abroad; whereby the imagery doth appear in figure; whereas in thoughts they lie but as in packs. Neither is this second fruit of friendship, in opening the understanding, restrained only to such friends as are able to give a man counsel; (they indeed are best;) but even without that, a man learneth of himself, and bringeth his own thoughts to light, and whetteth his wits as against a stone, which itself cuts not. In a word, a man were better relate himself to a statua, or picture, than to suffer his thoughts to pass in smother. Add now, to make this second fruit of friendship complete, that other point, which lieth more open, and falleth within vulgar observation; which is faithful counsel from a friend. Heraclitus saith well in one of his enigmas, Dry light is ever the best. And certain it is, that the light that a man receiveth by counsel from another, is drier and purer, than that which cometh from his own understanding and judgment; which is ever infused, and drenched, in his affections and customs. So as there is as much difference between the counsel, that a friend giveth, and that a man giveth himself, as there is between the counsel of a friend, and of a flatterer. For there is no such flatterer as is a man's self; and there is no such remedy against flattery of a man's self, as the liberty of a friend. Counsel is of two sorts: the one concerning manners, the other concerning business. For the first, the best preservative to keep the mind in health, is the faithful admonition of a friend. The calling of a man's self to a strict account, is a medicine, sometime too piercing and corrosive. Reading good books of morality, is a little flat and dead. Observing our faults in others, is sometimes improper for our case. But the best receipt (best, I say, to work, and best to take) is the admonition of a friend. It is a strange thing to behold, what gross errors and extreme absurdities many (especially of the greater sort) do commit, for want of a friend to tell them of them; to the great damage both of their fame and fortune: for, as St. James saith, they are as men that look sometimes into a glass, and presently forget their own shape and favor. As for business, a man may think, if he will, that two eyes see no more than one; or that a gamester seeth always more than a looker-on; or that a man in anger, is as wise as he that hath said over the four and twenty letters; or that a musket may be shot off as well upon the arm, as upon a rest; and such other fond and high imaginations, to think himself all in all. But when all is done, help of good counsel is that which setteth business straight. And if any man think that he will take counsel, but it shall be by pieces; asking counsel in one business, of one man, and in another business, of another man; it is well (that is to say, better, perhaps, than if he asked none at all); but he runneth two dangers: one, that he shall not be faithfully counselled; for it is a rare thing, except it be from a perfect and entire friend, to have counsel given, but such as shall be bowed and crooked to some ends, which he hath, that giveth it. The other, that he shall have counsel given, hurtful and unsafe (though with good meaning), and mixed partly of mischief and partly of remedy; even as if you would call a physician, that is thought good for the cure of the disease you complain of, but is unacquainted with your body; and therefore may put you in way for a present cure, but overthroweth your health in some other kind; and so cure the disease, and kill the patient. But a friend that is wholly acquainted with a man's estate, will beware, by furthering any present business, how he dasheth upon other inconvenience. And therefore rest not upon scattered counsels; they will rather distract and mislead, than settle and direct. After these two noble fruits of friendship (peace in the affections, and support of the judgment), followeth the last fruit; which is like the pomegranate, full of many kernels; I mean aid, and bearing a part, in all actions and occasions. Here the best way to represent to life the manifold use of friendship, is to cast and see how many things there are, which a man cannot do himself; and then it will appear, that it was a sparing speech of the ancients, to say, that a friend is another himself; for that a friend is far more than himself. Men have their time, and die many times, in desire of some things which they principally take to heart; the bestowing of a child, the finishing of a work, or the like. If a man have a true friend, he may rest almost secure that the care of those things will continue after him. So that a man hath, as it were, two lives in his desires. A man hath a body, and that body is confined to a place; but where friendship is, all offices of life are as it were granted to him, and his deputy. For he may exercise them by his friend. How many things are there which a man cannot, with any face or comeliness, say or do himself? A man can scarce allege his own merits with modesty, much less extol them; a man cannot sometimes brook to supplicate or beg;

and a number of the like. But all these things are graceful, in a friend's mouth, which are blushing in a man's own. So again, a man's person hath many proper relations, which he cannot put off. A man cannot speak to his son but as a father; to his wife but as a husband; to his enemy but upon terms: whereas a friend may speak as the case requires, and not as it sorteth with the person. But to enumerate these things were endless; I have given the rule, where a man cannot fitly play his own part; if he have not a friend, he may quit the stage.

Exercise

Of Friendship is one of Francis Bacon's most engaging explorations of human relationships. In this essay, Bacon reflects on the necessity and value of friendship in both personal and public life. He emphasizes that true friends provide not only emotional comfort but also intellectual clarity and practical support. Friendship, according to Bacon, serves as a remedy for solitude and a means of sharing one's joys and sorrows. He also highlights the role of friendship in enhancing wisdom, as friends act as mirrors that help us understand ourselves better. Beyond personal satisfaction, Bacon points out that friendship has social and political importance, strengthening bonds within communities and states.

I. Name your best friends.
II. Create a timeline of the best friends you had at different stages of your life and identify the qualities they possessed.
III. Choose a quote on friendship and write your views, opinions or comments.

Leisure

W. H. Davies

WHAT is this life if, full of care,
We have no time to stand and stare?—

No time to stand beneath the boughs,
And stare as long as sheep and cows:

No time to see, when woods we pass,
Where squirrels hide their nuts in grass:

No time to see, in broad daylight,
Streams full of stars, like skies at night:

No time to turn at Beauty's glance,
And watch her feet, how they can dance:

No time to wait till her mouth can
Enrich that smile her eyes began?

A poor life this if, full of care,
We have no time to stand and stare.

Exercise

'Leisure' is a reflective and thought-provoking piece that questions the fast pace of modern life. Written in simple yet lyrical language, the poem urges readers to slow down and appreciate the beauty of the natural world around them. Davies, who lived a life marked by both hardship and contemplation, draws attention to how people have become too busy to notice the small wonders that bring joy and peace. Through its rhythmic couplets and pastoral imagery, 'Leisure' serves as a gentle reminder of the importance of taking time to pause, observe, and reconnect with nature in an increasingly hurried world.

I. Write an argument on the topic: Life without leisure is dull and incomplete.
II. If you were given one extra hour today, what would you do with that hour?
III. List out your leisure time activities.

Anxiety Monster

Rhona McFerran

Anxiety, Anxiety –
you creep, you lurk, you worry me
Mangy monster under my bed
on all my fears you must be fed
and when I try to starve you out
you stab me with a blade of doubt

You sneaky, scurrilous, savage beast
I don't hate you, but I like you least!
You are not cute or cuddly
why do I let you cling to me?
You're ugly and you're worrisome
you drain my joy and leave me glum

Anxiety, Anxiety –
I hear you've achieved notoriety
evidently I'm not the only one
you'll hassle them all before you're done!
'Though, I don't see how you find the time
to carry out your heinous crime...

For all day long, and nighttime, too
a hovering pest, too big to "shoo"
you hang around and taunt me fierce
by dangling daggers with which to pierce
I tremble in my delicate skin
but chin stuck out, I'm determined to win

Anxiety, Anxiety –
you will not get the best of me!
You've wasted enough of my precious years
you deserve no sympathy or tears
like the monster you are, you'll be destroyed
I've armed myself with the likes of Freud

While you watch me, I'll study you more...
know your every weakness – for this is war!
I'll vanquish you for once and all
I've armored up for the bloody brawl
but hey – what's this, a hasty retreat?
Don't tell me that you admit defeat!

No Anxiety, Anxiety –
you're devious, sly and slippery
Before you let me kill you off
you slink away to smirk and scoff
knowing full well that you'll come back
to get me with a sneak-attack!

Exercise

The poem *Anxiety Monster* describes anxiety as an ever-present creature that follows the speaker throughout their day and mind. It is portrayed as sneaky, persistent, and draining whispering doubts, feeding fear, and growing stronger. Despite the monster's presence, the speaker often tries to hide its existence or struggle with it silently. The monster is depicted as relentless and intrusive, creeping into the speaker's life without invitation. It whispers doubts, amplifies worries, and feeds on the speaker's insecurities. The poem ends with a note of resilience, self-awareness, and a call to face the monster with compassion or courage.

I. Write a conversation between you and a friend who is stressed out to find a solution to overcome anxiety.
II. Enumerate the strategies or techniques you use to manage anxiety, and explain how effective they were.
III. Write some tips to replace negative thoughts with positive thinking.

On the Rule of the Road

A. G. Gardiner

That was a jolly story which Mr. Arthur Ransome told the other day in one of his messages from Petrograd. A stout old lady was walking with her basket down the middle of a street in Petrograd to the great confusion of the traffic and with no small peril to herself. It was pointed out to her that the pavement was the place for foot-passengers, but she replied: "I'm going to walk where I like. We've got liberty now." It did not occur to the dear old lady that if liberty entitled the foot-passenger to walk down the middle of the road it also entitled the cab-driver to drive on the pavement, and that the end of such liberty would be universal chaos. Everybody would be getting in everybody else's way and nobody would get anywhere. Individual liberty would have become social anarchy.

There is a danger of the world getting liberty-drunk in these days like the old lady with the basket, and it is just as well to remind ourselves of what the rule of the road means. It means that in order that the liberties of all may be preserved the liberties of everybody must be curtailed. When the policeman, say, at Piccadilly Circus steps into the middle of the road and puts up his hand, he is the symbol not of tyranny, but of liberty. You may not think so. You may, being in a hurry and seeing your motor-car pulled up by this insolence of office, feel that your liberty has been outraged. How dare this fellow interfere with your free use of the public highway? Then, if you are a reasonable person, you will reflect that if he did not, incidentally, interfere with you he would interfere with no one, and the result would be that Piccadilly Circus would be a maelstrom that you would never cross at all. You have submitted to a curtailment of private liberty in order that you may enjoy a social order which makes your liberty a reality.

Liberty is not a personal affair only, but a social contract. It is an accommodation of interests. In matters which do not touch anybody else's liberty, of course, I may be as free as I like. If I choose to go down the Strand in a dressing-gown, with long hair and bare feet, who shall say me nay? You have liberty to laugh at me, but I have liberty to be indifferent to you. And if I have a fancy for dyeing my hair, or waxing my moustache (which heaven forbid), or wearing a tall hat, a frock-coat and sandals, or going to bed late or getting up early, I shall follow my fancy and ask no man's permission. I shall not inquire of you whether I may eat mustard with my mutton. I may like mustard with my mutton. And you will not ask me whether you may be a Protestant or a Catholic, whether you may marry the dark lady or the fair lady, whether you may prefer Ella Wheeler Wilcox to Wordsworth, or champagne to shandygaff.

In all these and a thousand other details you and I please ourselves and ask no one's leave. We have a whole kingdom in which we rule alone, can do what we choose, be wise or ridiculous, harsh or easy, conventional or odd. But directly we step out of that kingdom our personal liberty of action becomes qualified by other people's liberty. I might like to practise on the trombone from midnight till three in the morning. If I went on to the top of Helvellyn to do it I could please myself, but if I do it in my bedroom my family will object, and if I do it out in the streets the neighbours will remind me that my liberty to blow the trombone must not interfere with their liberty to sleep in quiet. There are a lot of people in the world, and I have to accommodate my liberty to their liberties.

We are all liable to forget this, and unfortunately we are much more conscious of the imperfections of others in this respect than of our own.

I got into a railway carriage at a country station the other morning and settled down for what the schoolboys would call an hour's "swot" at a Blue-book. I was not reading it for pleasure. The truth is that I never do read Blue-books for pleasure. I read them as a barrister reads a brief, for the very humble purpose of turning an honest penny out of them. Now, if you are reading a book for pleasure it doesn't matter what is going on around you. I think I could enjoy "Tristram Shandy" or "Treasure Island" in the midst of an earthquake.

But when you are reading a thing as a task you need reasonable quiet, and that is what I didn't get, for at the next station in came a couple of men, one of whom talked to his friend for the rest of the journey in a loud and pompous voice. He was one of those people who remind one of that story of Home Tooke who, meeting a person of immense swagger in the street, stopped him and said, "Excuse me, sir, but are you someone in particular?" This gentleman was someone in particular. As I wrestled with clauses and sections, his voice rose like a gale, and his family history, the deeds of his sons in the war, and his criticisms of the generals and the politicians submerged my poor attempts to hang on to my job. I shut up the Blue-book, looked out of the window, and listened wearily while the voice thundered on with themes like these: "Now what French ought to have done..." "The mistake the Germans made..." "If only Asquith had..." You know the sort of stuff. I had heard it all before, oh, so often. It was like a barrel-organ groaning out some banal song of long ago.

If I had asked him to be good enough to talk in a lower tone I daresay he would have thought I was a very rude fellow. It did not occur to him that anybody could have anything better to do than to listen to him, and I have no doubt he left the carriage convinced that everybody in it had, thanks to him, had a very illuminating journey, and would carry away a pleasing impression of his encyclopædic range. He was obviously a well-intentioned person.

The thing that was wrong with him was that he had not the social sense. He was not "a clubbable man."

A reasonable consideration for the rights or feelings of others is the foundation of social conduct. It is commonly alleged against women that in this respect they are less civilised than men, and I am bound to confess that in my experience it is the woman – the well-dressed woman – who thrusts herself in front of you at the ticket office. The man would not attempt it, partly because he knows the thing would not be tolerated from him, but also because he has been better drilled in the small give-and-take of social relationships. He has lived more in the broad current of the world, where you have to learn to accommodate yourself to the general standard of conduct, and his school life, his club life, and his games have in this respect given him a training that women are only now beginning to enjoy.

I believe that the rights of small people and quiet people are as important to preserve as the rights of small nationalities. When I hear the aggressive, bullying horn which some motorists deliberately use, I confess that I feel something boiling up in me which is very like what I felt when Germany came trampling like a bully over Belgium. By what right, my dear sir, do you go along our highways uttering that hideous curse on all who impede your path? Cannot you announce your coming like a gentleman? Cannot you take your turn? Are you someone in particular or are you simply a hot gospeller of the prophet Nietzsche? I find myself wondering what sort of a person it is who can sit behind that hog-like outrage without realising that he is the spirit of Prussia incarnate, and a very ugly spectacle in a civilised world.

And there is the more harmless person who has bought a very blatant gramophone, and on Sunday afternoon sets the thing going, opens the windows and fills the street with "Keep the Home Fires Burning" or some similar banality. What are the right limits of social behaviour in a matter of this sort? Let us take the trombone as an illustration again. Hazlitt said that a man who wanted to learn that fearsome instrument was entitled to learn it in his own house, even though he was a nuisance to his neighbours, but it was his business to make the nuisance as slight as possible. He must practise in the attic, and shut the window. He had no right to sit in his front room, open the window, and blow his noise into his neighbours' ears with the maximum of violence. And so with the gramophone. If you like the gramophone you are entitled to have it, but you are interfering with the liberties of your neighbours if you don't do what you can to limit the noise to your own household. Your neighbours may not like "Keep the Home Fires Burning." They may prefer to have their Sunday afternoon undisturbed, and it is as great an impertinence for you to wilfully trespass on their peace as it would be to go, unasked, into their gardens and trample on their flower beds.

There are cases, of course, where the clash of liberties seems to defy compromise. My dear old friend X., who lives in a West End square and who is an amazing mixture of good nature and irascibility, flies into a passion when he hears a street piano, and rushes out to order it away. But near by lives a distinguished lady of romantic picaresque tastes, who dotes on street pianos, and attracts them as wasps are attracted to a jar of jam. Whose liberty in this case should surrender to the other? For the life of me I cannot say. It is as reasonable to like street pianos as to dislike them – and vice versa. I would give much to hear Sancho Panza's solution of such a nice riddle.

I suppose the fact is that we can be neither complete anarchists nor complete Socialists in this complex world – or rather we must be a judicious mixture of both. We have both liberties to preserve – our individual liberty and our social liberty. We must watch the bureaucrat on the one side and warn off the anarchist on the other. I am neither a Marxist, nor a Tolstoyan, but a compromise. I shall not permit any authority to say that my child must go to this school or that, shall specialise in science or arts, shall play rugger or soccer. These things are personal. But if I proceed to say that my child shall have no education at all, that he shall be brought up as a primeval savage, or at Mr. Fagin's academy for pickpockets, then Society will politely but firmly tell me that it has no use for primeval savages and a very stern objection to pickpockets, and that my child must have a certain minimum of education whether I like it or not. I cannot have the liberty to be a nuisance to my neighbours or make my child a burden and a danger to the commonwealth.

It is in the small matters of conduct, in the observance of the rule of the road, that we pass judgment upon ourselves, and declare that we are civilised or uncivilised. The great moments of heroism and sacrifice are rare. It is the little habits of commonplace intercourse that make up the great sum of life and sweeten or make bitter the journey. I hope my friend in the railway carriage will reflect on this. Then he will not cease, I am sure, to explain to his neighbour where French went wrong and where the Germans went ditto; but he will do it in a way that will permit me to read my Blue-book undisturbed.

Exercises

On the Rule of the Road by A.G. Gardiner is a witty and thought-provoking essay that explores the delicate balance between individual liberty and social order. Using the simple metaphor of traffic rules, Gardiner illustrates how true freedom often means the willingness to restrain oneself for the greater good. With charm and clarity, he reminds us that civilized life depends not just on rights, but on responsibilities – a lesson as relevant on the road as it is in society at large.

I. Analyse the **graphic organizer** of the Fundamental Rights from the Constitution of India under the lens of **Expression of Freedom** and **Limitations of Personal Freedom**. The right to equality is given an example. Provide examples for the other rights.

Constitution of India – Fundamental Rights

Fundamental Right	*Expression of Freedom*	*Limitations of Personal Freedom*	*Examples*
Right to Equality	Equality before law, equal protection of laws, no discrimination, equal opportunities in employment.	Special provisions for women, children, socially and educationally backward classes allowed as exceptions (reservation policies).	A woman cannot be denied a job because of her gender.

Fundamental Right	*Expression of Freedom*	*Limitations of Personal Freedom*	*Examples*
Right to Freedom	Freedom of speech and expression, assembly, association, movement, residence, profession.	Subject to restrictions for sovereignty, integrity of India, security of state, friendly relations with foreign states, public order, morality, decency.	
Right against Exploitation	Freedom from human trafficking, bonded labour, and child labour.	Children below 14 cannot be employed in hazardous industries, even if parents consent.	
Right to Freedom of Religion	Freedom of conscience; right to profess, practice, and propagate religion.	Restrictions in the interest of public order, morality, health, or other fundamental rights.	
Cultural & Educational Rights	Right to preserve language, script, culture; minorities can establish educational institutions.	Subject to maintaining national interest and educational standards.	
Right to Constitutional Remedies	Right to move Supreme Court/High Courts to protect fundamental rights.	Courts can dismiss frivolous petitions or impose reasonable restrictions.	

II. Write about any one of the following:
- Conversational Etiquette
- Classroom Etiquette
- Table Etiquette
- Social Media Etiquette

III. Write about the importance of the magic words in daily life:
- "Please"
- "Thank you"
- "I'm sorry"
- "Excuse me"
- "You're welcome"

And Still I Rise

Maya Angelou

You may write me down in history
With your bitter, twisted lies,
You may trod me in the very dirt
But still, like dust, I'll rise.

Does my sassiness upset you?
Why are you beset with gloom?
'Cause I walk like I've got oil wells
Pumping in my living room.

Just like moons and like suns,
With the certainty of tides,
Just like hopes springing high,
Still I'll rise.

Did you want to see me broken?
Bowed head and lowered eyes?
Shoulders falling down like teardrops,
Weakened by my soulful cries?

Does my haughtiness offend you?
Don't you take it awful hard
'Cause I laugh like I've got gold mines
Diggin' in my own backyard.

You may shoot me with your words,
You may cut me with your eyes,
You may kill me with your hatefulness,
But still, like air, I'll rise.

Does my sexiness upset you?
Does it come as a surprise
That I dance like I've got diamonds
At the meeting of my thighs?

Out of the huts of history's shame
I rise
Up from a past that's rooted in pain
I rise
I'm a black ocean, leaping and wide,
Welling and swelling I bear in the tide.

Leaving behind nights of terror and fear
I rise
Into a daybreak that's wondrously clear
I rise
Bringing the gifts that my ancestors gave,
I am the dream and the hope of the slave.
I rise
I rise
I rise.

Exercise

This powerful poem by Maya Angelou is a celebration of strength, hope, and resilience in the face of oppression. With a confident and defiant tone, the speaker refuses to be broken by racism, sexism, or injustice. The poem uses repetition and vivid imagery to affirm the enduring spirit of Black identity and pride. *And Still I Rise* inspires readers to rise above difficulties with courage and dignity.

I. Identify the issues that women face related to education, work, healthcare, legal rights, and violence. Elaborate on any one of the rights of women related to the issue.

II. Write a short poem/compose a song/ a skit about how you overcame a difficulty or criticism, with confidence.

III. Write few slogans against discrimination based on colour, caste or creed.

SEMESTER IV

We Real Cool

Gwendolyn Brooks

The Pool Players.
Seven at the Golden Shovel.

We real cool. We
Left school. We

Lurk late. We
Strike straight. We

Sing sin. We
Thin gin. We

Jazz June. We
Die soon.

Exercise

In "We Real Cool," Gwendolyn Brooks captures how small choices like skipping school or staying out late can lead to powerful consequences, ultimately ending in the haunting line: "We die soon." The poem's minimalist style and sharp compact lines reflect how even the smallest shifts in life can carry deep meaning.

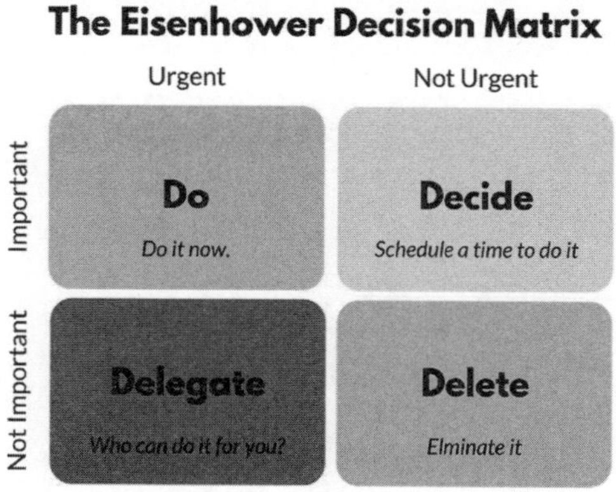

I. Priortize your tasks that are urgent and most important based on Eisenhower Matrix.
II. Create a Poetry wall in the classroom with inspirational lines chosen from poems.
III. A word ladder is a simple, thought-provoking game which shows how subtle changes can lead to entirely new outcomes, where one word gets transformed into another, changing just one letter at a time.

Brooks invites us to reflect on life's turning points through carefully chosen words in the poem, the word ladder too challenges us to explore transformation in language—one letter at a time, each step must form a valid English word.

Word Ladder Example: **Create a ladder Head – Tail**

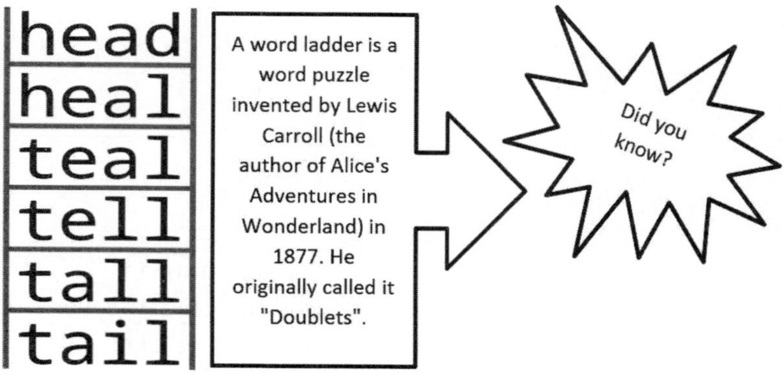

- Word Ladder 1 – Fill in the missing letters to create word ladder **Log – man**
- Word Ladder 2 - Follow the clue images and create word ladder **Cup – Bug**
- Word Ladder 3 – Follow the clue words and create word ladder **Cold – Farm**

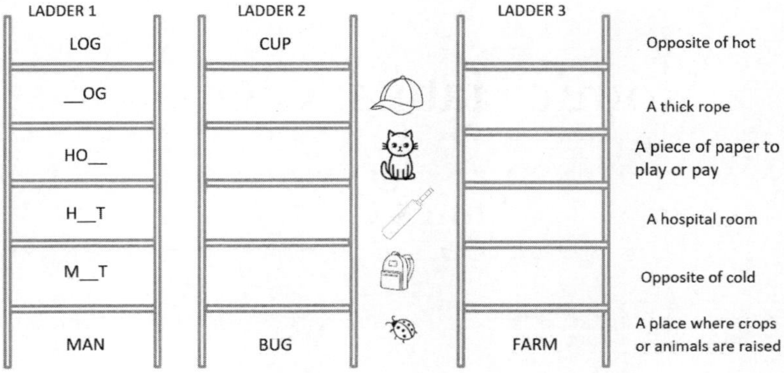

Atomic Habits: Chapter 2

James Clear

How Your Habits Shape Your Identity (and vice versa)

Why is it so easy to repeat bad habits and so hard to form good ones? Few things can have a more powerful impact on your life than improving your daily habits. And yet it is likely that this time next year you'll be doing the same thing rather than something better.

It often feels difficult to keep good habits going for more than a few days, even with sincere effort and the occasional burst of motivation. Habits like exercise, meditation, journaling, and cooking are reasonable for a day or two and then become a hassle.

However, once your habits are established, they seem to stick around forever—especially the unwanted ones. Despite our best intentions, unhealthy habits like eating junk food, watching too much television, procrastinating, and smoking can feel impossible to break.

Changing our habits is challenging for two reasons: (1) we try to change the wrong thing and (2) we try to change our habits in the wrong way. In this chapter, I'll address the first point. In the chapters that follow, I'll answer the second.

Our first mistake is that we try to change the wrong thing. To understand what I mean, consider that there are three levels at which change can occur. You can imagine them like the layers of an onion.

Three Layers of Behavior Change

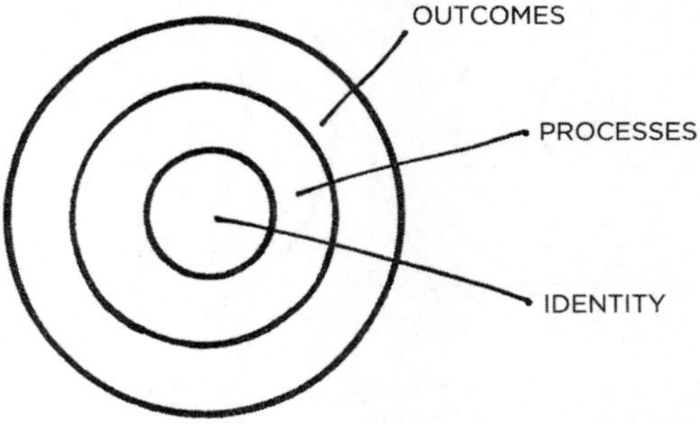

Figure: There are three layers of behavior change:
A change in your outcomes, a change in your processes,
or a change in your identity.

The first layer is changing your outcomes. This level is concerned with changingyour results: losing weight, publishing a book, winning a championship. Most of the goals you set are associated with this level of change. The second layer is changing your process. This level is concerned with changing your habits and systems: implementing a new routine at the gym, decluttering your desk for better workflow, developing a meditation practice. Most of the habits you build are associated with this level.

The third and deepest layer is changing your identity. This level is concerned with changing your beliefs: your worldview, your self-image, your judgments about yourself and others. Most of the beliefs, assumptions, and biases you hold are associated with this level.

Outcomes are about what you get. Processes are about what you do. Identity is about what you believe. When it comes to building habits that last—when it comes to building a system of 1 percent improvements—the problem is not that one level is "better" or "worse" than another. All levels of change are useful in their own way. The problem is the *direction* of change.

Many people begin the process of changing their habits by focusing on *what* they want to achieve. This leads us to outcome-based habits. The alternative is to build identity-based habits. With this approach, we start by focusing on *who* we wish to become.

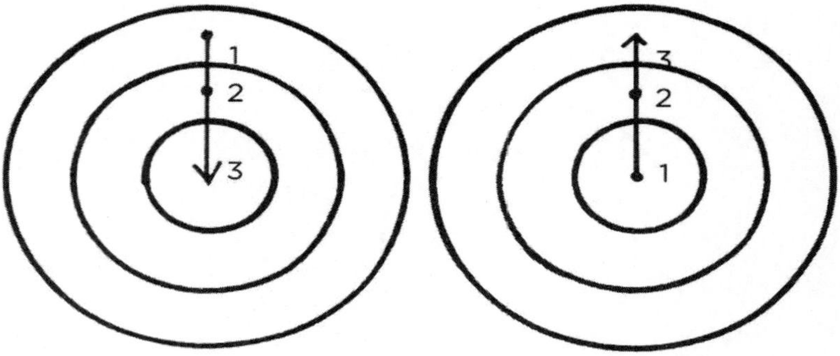

Outcome-based Habits Identity-based Habits

Figure: With outcome-based habits, the focus is on what you want to achieve. With identity-based habits, the focus is on who you wish to become.

Imagine two people resisting a cigarette. When offered a smoke, the first person says, "No thanks. I'm trying to quit." It sounds like a reasonable response, but this person still believes they are a smoker who is trying to be something else. They are hoping their behavior will change while carrying around the same beliefs.

The second person declines by saying, "No thanks. I'm not a smoker." It's a small difference, but this statement signals a shift in identity. Smoking was part of their former life, not their current one. They no longer identify as someone who smokes.

Most people don't even consider identity change when they set out to improve. They just think, "I want to be skinny (outcome) and if I stick to this diet, then I'll be skinny (process)." They set goals and determine the actions they should take to achieve those goals without considering the beliefs that drive their actions. They never shift the way they look at themselves, and they don't realize that their old identity can sabotage their new plans for change.

Behind every system of actions are a system of beliefs. The system of a democracy is founded on beliefs like freedom, majority rule, and social equality. The system of a dictatorship has a very different set of beliefs like absolute authority and strict obedience. You can imagine many ways to try to get more people to vote in a democracy, but such behavior change would never get off the ground in a dictatorship. That's not the identity of the system. Voting is a behavior that is impossible under a certain set of beliefs.

A similar pattern exists whether we are discussing individuals, organizations, or societies. There are a set of beliefs and assumptions that shape the system, an identity behind the habits.

Behavior that is incongruent with the self will not last. You may want more money, but if your identity is someone who consumes rather than creates, then you'll continue to be pulled toward spending rather than earning. You may want better health, but if you continue to prioritize comfort over accomplishment, you'll be drawn to relaxing rather than training. It's hard to change your habits if you never change the underlying beliefs that led to your past behavior. You have a new goal and a new plan, but you haven't changed *who* you are.

The story of Brian Clark, an entrepreneur from Boulder, Colorado, provides a good example. "For as long as I can remember, I've chewed my fingernails," Clark told me. "It started as a nervous habit when I was young, and then morphed into an undesirable grooming ritual. One day, I resolved to stop chewing my nails until they grew out a bit. Through mindful willpower alone, I managed to do it."

Then, Clark did something surprising.

"I asked my wife to schedule my first-ever manicure," he said. "My thought was that if I started paying to maintain my nails, I wouldn't chew them. And it worked, but not for the monetary reason. What happened was the manicure made my fingers look really nice for the first time. The manicurist even said that— other than the chewing—I had really healthy, attractive nails. Suddenly, I was proud of my fingernails. And even though that's something I had never aspired to, it made all the difference. I've never chewed my nails since; not even a single close call. And it's because I now take pride in properly caring for them."

The ultimate form of intrinsic motivation is when a habit becomes part of your identity. It's one thing to say I'm the type of person who wants this. It's something very different to say I'm the type of person who is this.

The more pride you have in a particular aspect of your identity, the more motivated you will be to maintain the habits associated with it. If you're proud of how your hair looks, you'll develop all sorts of habits to care for and maintain it. If you're proud of the size of your biceps, you'll make sure you never skip an upper-body workout. If you're proud of the scarves you knit, you'll be more likely to spend hours knitting each week. Once your pride gets involved, you'll fight tooth and nail to maintain your habits.

True behavior change is identity change. You might start a habit because of motivation, but the only reason you'll stick with one is that it becomes part of your identity. Anyone can convince themselves to visit the gym or eat healthy once or twice, but if you don't shift the belief behind the behavior, then it is hard to stick with long-term changes. Improvements are only temporary until they become part of who you are.

- The goal is not to read a book, the goal is to *become* a reader.
- The goal is not to run a marathon, the goal is to *become* a runner.
- The goal is not to learn an instrument, the goal is to *become* a musician.

Your behaviors are usually a reflection of your identity. What you do is an indication of the type of person you believe that you are—either consciously or nonconsciously. Research has shown that once a person believes in a particular aspect of their identity, they are more likely to act in alignment with that belief. For example, people who identified as "being a voter" were more likely to vote than those who simply claimed "voting" was an action they wanted to perform. Similarly, the person who incorporates exercise into their identity doesn't have to convince themselves to train. Doing the right thing is easy. After all, when your behavior and your identity are fully aligned, you are no longer pursuing behavior change. You are simply acting like the type of person you already believe yourself to be.

Like all aspects of habit formation, this, too, is a double-edged sword. When working for you, identity change can be a powerful force for self improvement. When working against you, though, identity change can be a curse. Once you have adopted an identity, it can be easy to let your allegiance to it impact your ability to change. Many people walk through life in a cognitive slumber, blindly following the norms attached to their identity.

- "I'm terrible with directions."
- "I'm not a morning person."
- "I'm bad at remembering people's names."
- "I'm always late."
- "I'm not good with technology."
- "I'm horrible at math."

. . . and a thousand other variations.

When you have repeated a story to yourself for years, it is easy to slide into these mental grooves and accept them as a fact. In time, you begin to resist certain actions because "that's not who I am." There is internal pressure to maintain your self-image and behave in a way that is consistent with your beliefs. You find whatever way you can to avoid contradicting yourself.

The more deeply a thought or action is tied to your identity, the more difficult it is to change it. It can feel comfortable to believe what your culture believes (group identity) or to do what upholds your self-image (personal identity), even if it's wrong. The biggest barrier to positive change at any level—individual, team, society—is identity conflict. Good habits can make rational sense, but if they conflict with your identity, you will fail to put them into action.

On any given day, you may struggle with your habits because you're too busy or too tired or too overwhelmed or hundreds of other reasons. Over the long run, however, the real reason you fail to stick with habits is that your self-image gets in the way. This is why you can't get too attached to one version of your identity. Progress requires unlearning. Becoming the best version of yourself requires you to continuously edit your beliefs, and to upgrade and expand your identity.

This brings us to an important question: If your beliefs and worldview play such an important role in your behavior, where do they come from in the first place? How, exactly, is your identity formed? And how can you emphasize new aspects of your identity that serve you and gradually erase the pieces that hinder you?

The Two-Step Process to Changing Your Identity

Your identity emerges out of your habits. You are not born with preset beliefs. Every belief, including those about yourself, is learned and conditioned through experience.

More precisely, your habits are how you *embody* your identity. When you make your bed each day, you embody the identity of an organized person. When you write each day, you embody the identity of a creative person. When you train each day, you embody the identity of an athletic person.

The more you repeat a behavior, the more you reinforce the identity associated with that behavior. In fact, the word *identity* was originally derived from the Latin words *essentitas*, which means *being*, and *identidem*, which means *repeatedly*. Your identity is literally your "repeated beingness."

Whatever your identity is right now, you only believe it because you have proof of it. If you go to church every Sunday for twenty years, you have evidence that you are religious. If you study biology for one hour every night, you have evidence that you are studious. If you go to the gym even when it's snowing, you have evidence that you are committed to fitness. The more evidence you have for a belief, the more strongly you will believe it.

For most of my early life, I didn't consider myself a writer. If you were to ask any of my high school teachers or college professors, they would tell you I was an average writer at best: certainly not a standout. When I began my writing career, I published a new article every Monday and Thursday for the first few years. As the evidence grew, so did my identity as a writer. I didn't start out as a writer. I *became* one through my habits.

Of course, your habits are not the *only* actions that influence your identity, but by virtue of their frequency they are usually the most important ones. Each experience in life modifies your self-image, but it's unlikely you would consider yourself a soccer player because you kicked a ball once or an artist because you scribbled a picture. As you repeat these actions, however, the evidence accumulates and your self-image begins to change. The effect of one-off experiences tends to fade away while the effect of habits gets reinforced with time, which means your habits contribute most of the evidence that shapes your identity. In this way, the process of building habits is actually the process of becoming yourself.

This is a gradual evolution. We do not change by snapping our fingers and deciding to be someone entirely new. We change bit by bit, day by day, habit by habit. We are continually undergoing microevolutions of the self.

Each habit is like a suggestion: "Hey, maybe *this* is who I am." If you finish a book, then perhaps you are the type of person who likes reading. If you go to the gym, then perhaps you are the type of person who likes exercise. If you practice playing the guitar, perhaps you are the type of person who likes music.

Every action you take is a vote for the type of person you wish to become. No single instance will transform your beliefs, but as the votes build up, so does the evidence of your new identity.This is one reason why meaningful change does not require radical change. Small habits can make a meaningful difference by providing evidence of a new identity. And if a change is meaningful, it actually is big. That's the paradox of making small improvements.

Putting this all together, you can see that habits are the path to changing your identity. The most practical way to change *who* you are is to change *what* you do.

- Each time you write a page, you are a writer.
- Each time you practice the violin, you are a musician.
- Each time you start a workout, you are an athlete.
- Each time you encourage your employees, you are a leader.

Each habit not only gets results but also teaches you something far more important: to trust yourself. You start to believe you can actually accomplish these things. When the votes mount up and the evidence begins to change, the story you tell yourself begins to change as well.

Of course, it works the opposite way, too. Every time you choose to perform a bad habit, it's a vote for that identity. The good news is that you don't need to be perfect. In any election, there are going to be votes for both sides. You don't need a unanimous vote to win an election; you just need a majority. It doesn't matter if you cast a few votes for a bad behavior or an unproductive habit. Your goal is simply to win the majority of the time.

New identities require new evidence. If you keep casting the same votes you've always cast, you're going to get the same results you've always had. If nothing changes, nothing is going to change.

It is a simple two-step process:

1. Decide the type of person you want to be.
2. Prove it to yourself with small wins.

First, decide who you want to be. This holds at any level—as an individual, as a team, as a community, as a nation. What do you want to stand for? What are your principles and values? Who do you wish to become?

These are big questions, and many people aren't sure where to begin—but they do know what kind of results they want: to get six-pack abs or to feel less anxious or to double their salary. That's fine. Start there and work backward from the results you want to the type of person who could get those results. Ask yourself, "Who is the type of person that could get the outcome I want?" Who is the type of person that could lose forty pounds? Who is the type of person that could learn a new language? Who is the type of person that could run a successful start-up?

For example, "Who is the type of person who could write a book?" It's probably someone who is consistent and reliable. Now your focus shifts from writing a book (outcome-based) to being the type of person who is consistent and reliable (identity-based).

This process can lead to beliefs like:

- "I'm the kind of teacher who stands up for her students."
- "I'm the kind of doctor who gives each patient the time and empathy they need."
- "I'm the kind of manager who advocates for her employees."

Once you have a handle on the type of person you want to be, you can begin taking small steps to reinforce your desired identity. I have a friend who lost over 100 pounds by asking herself, "What would a healthy person do?" All day long, she would use this question as a guide. Would a healthy person walk or take a cab? Would a healthy person order a burrito or a salad? She figured if she acted like a healthy person long enough, eventually she would become that person. She was right.

The concept of identity-based habits is our first introduction to another key theme in this book: feedback loops. Your habits shape your identity, and your identity shapes your habits. It's a two-way street. The formation of all habits is a feedback loop (a concept we will explore in depth in the next chapter), but it's important to let your values, principles, and identity drive the loop rather than your results. The focus should always be on becoming that type of person, not getting a particular outcome.

The Real Reason Habits Matter

Identity change is the North Star of habit change. The remainder of this book will provide you with step-by-step instructions on how to build better habits in yourself, your family, your team, your company, and anywhere else you wish.

But the true question is: "Are you becoming the type of person you want to become?" The first step is not *what* or *how*, but *who*. You need to know who you want to be. Otherwise, your quest for change is like a boat without a rudder. And that's why we are starting here.

You have the power to change your beliefs about yourself. Your identity is not set in stone. You have a choice in every moment. You can choose the identity you want to reinforce today with the habits you choose today. And this brings us to the deeper purpose of this book and the real reason habits matter.

Building better habits isn't about littering your day with life hacks. It's not about flossing one tooth each night or taking a cold shower each morning or wearing the same outfit each day. It's not about achieving external measures of success like earning more money, losing weight, or reducing stress. Habits can help you achieve all of these things, but fundamentally they are not about having something. They are about becoming someone.

Ultimately, your habits matter because they help you become the type of person you wish to be. They are the channel through which you develop your deepest beliefs about yourself. Quite literally, you become your habits.

Exercise

The chapter 2 of Atomic Habits looks at how habits affect our sense of identity. It explains that true and lasting change happens when we focus on who we want to be instead of just what we want to accomplish. James Clear introduces the idea of identity-based habits, which can help people make meaningful changes in their lives. He is a writer and speaker known for his expertise in habit formation, decision-making, and continuous improvement. Atomic Habits is his best-selling book on personal development.

I. Tiny habits can bring massive change. Even the smallest consistent actions can reshape life—transforming the character, personality, emotions, thoughts, and expanding one's capacity. Over time, they boost productivity, strength, and overall impact.

   Use the habit tracker model and guiding questions below to kick-start a powerful new habit.

   When choosing a habit to develop, be **SMART**:

   - **Specific** – Clearly define the habit you want to build
   - **Measurable** – Ensure you can track your progress
   - **Achievable** – Start with something small and realistic
   - **Relevant** – Pick a habit that supports your personal growth and goals
   - **Time-Bound** – Set a clear timeframe to practice and evaluate it

   List three positive habits to start

   (a) ____

(b) ____

(c) ____

II. Schedule the new habits:
Assign your new habits a specific time and place in your daily schedule:

III. Use the following habit tracker for 7 days and continue it for 90 days to make the habit a part of your life. (check the box and rate yourself on completing the task):

	Day 1	*Day 2*	*Day 3*	*Day 4*	*Day 5*	*Day 6*	*Day 7*	*Rate 1-10*	*Reward*
New habit 1									
New habit 2									
New habit 3									

The Giant's Wife: A Tall Tale of Ireland

William Carleton

NARRATOR 1: Many years ago in the north of Ireland, there lived a giant named Fin MacCool.

FIN: *(proudly, to audience)* That's me name!

NARRATOR 4: One thing Fin is said to have done was to make a road that crossed the sea from Ireland to Scotland. You can still see what's supposed to be the first stretch of that road. It's called the Giant's Causeway, and it's a group of great rocks all fitting together.

NARRATOR 2: Now, this story happened when Fin was *building* his road. At the time we're talking about, Fin was a worried giant. He'd been told that another giant, called Cuhullin, was looking for him to challenge him to a fight, to find out which of them was the strongest.

CUHULLIN: *(growls, to audience)*

NARRATOR 3: This Cuhullin was said to have beaten every giant in Ireland except Fin, and the thought of meeting him face to face made Fin shake in his boots.

NARRATOR 1: Well, when Fin had been working away from home a good many months, he took it into his head to go home and see his wife, a fine woman named Oona. It was two counties away—but sure that wasn't far for a man like Fin.

NARRATOR 4: He pulled up a fir tree by its roots—a *fullgrown* tree, mind you—and stripped off the branches to make himself a walking stick. Then off he set, and in no time at all he reached his own mountain and the house he'd built on it, and there was Oona to greet him.

FIN: *(heartily, with arms outstretched)* Oona, me love!

OONA: *(warmly)* Ach, Fin, it's glad I am to see you. I hope you're a bit hungry, for I fixed a little something when I saw you coming.

NARRATOR 2: She sat him down to a grand meal of three whole roast oxen, thirty boiled cabbages, and a pile of her best bread loaves, which she'd just taken from the oven.

FIN: *(starts eating)* A finer cook never filled this great belly! *(keeps eating, but distractedly)*

NARRATOR 3: But Oona could see that her husband was worried about something.

OONA: What ails you, Fin?

FIN: Ach, Oona, it's this Cuhullin.

NARRATOR 1: Fin told her how the dreaded giant was looking for him.

FIN: And every time I suck me thumb, I get more worried about him.

NARRATOR 4: You see, Fin had a magic thumb, and if he sucked it, it would warn him of any danger.

NARRATOR 2: Now, Oona was worried too, but she had an idea.

OONA: Go now, and look across the mountain for his coming. You're sure to see him on his way, and that'll give us time to prepare a welcome.

NARRATOR 3: So Fin MacCool did what his wife bid, for he knew her to be a woman of great good sense. And inside the house, Oona cleared the table and began baking a new batch of bread loaves. These were the big, flat loaves you can see in Ireland to this day. But this was a special batch indeed, for inside each loaf she put a great iron griddle.

NARRATOR 1: Well, at last Fin ran into the house.

FIN: Oona, he's coming, and he's a terrible size of a creature! What can I do? If I run away, I'll be shamed forever! And if I stay here, he'll tie my body in knots!

OONA: Ach, be easy now, Fin. Just do what I say, and before the day is out, maybe his own forefinger will betray him. *(goes to the other room)*

NARRATOR 4: You see, Cuhullin too had a magic finger. All his strength was in the forefinger of his right hand. If he lost that finger, he'd be no stronger than any ordinary man.

FIN: *(looking out the open door)* He's coming! He'll be here in a minute!

OONA: *(comes back)* Now, hold your tongue, Fin, and put on this nightgown of mine.

FIN: *(indignantly)* What?! Me put on the clothes of a woman?! Are you trying to make a fool of me?

OONA: Trust me, now, Fin.

FIN: *(glares at her stubbornly, then gives in with a sigh)*

NARRATOR 2: So, grumbling away, Fin put on his wife's nightgown. Oona put a white bonnet on his head, then pushed him toward a cradle in the corner.

FIN: Woman, what do you think you're doing?!

OONA: *(pushing him into the cradle)* Just lie down there, Fin. And you'll need this baby bottle too. *(sticks the bottle in FIN's mouth)*

FIN: *(opening his eyes wide as he gets the bottle)* Ulp!

OONA: Now, keep yourself quiet and leave everything to me.

NARRATOR 3: Just then, Cuhullin came walking up fast to the house.

CUHULLIN: *(stopping at the doorway and speaking gruffly to OONA)* Good day to you.

OONA: *(coming forward cheerily)* Come in, then, and welcome! 'Twill grieve my husband to know you called when he wasn't here to greet you.

CUHULLIN: *(coming in)* Well, now, that's very civil of you, woman. But it grieves me even more to learn he's not at home, 'cause I was told I'd find him here.

OONA: Well, now, you were told wrong, for Fin is away at his causeway. He went rushing there in a terrible rage. It seems that some giant called Cuhullin has been looking for him, and Fin went off to teach that fool a lesson.

CUHULLIN: Then I'll go and find him there, for *I'm* Cuhullin, and I won't rest till I've settled any argument about whether he's stronger than me.

OONA: Ach, don't be in such a hurry. Come in and take your rest awhile. You'll need it, if it's *Fin* you're going to fight, for he's twice your size and ten times stronger-looking!

FIN: (*gasps, taking the bottle from his mouth)*

NARRATOR 1: Fin nearly fell out of the cradle with fright.

FIN: *(in dismay, softly to himself)* Oh, why does she have to go and blab like that? Why doesn't she just let him go?

NARRATOR 4: But Oona wasn't so anxious to get rid of Cuhullin.

OONA: Now, just set yourself down, and I'll have a meal ready for you in no time. I've got the bread all baked and a lovely pot of stew on the fire. *(turns to go, then turns back)* Oh, while you're waiting, I wonder if you'd do me a favor. A cold wind blows in at the door, this time of day. Would you be so kind as to turn the house around? Fin always does it for me when he's home.

CUHULLIN: Certainly.

NARRATOR 2: Up he got and went outside. With no bother at all, he picked up the whole house and turned it to face the other way.

NARRATOR 3: Oona was a bit surprised, because Fin himself couldn't have done it—she'd just made that up to frighten Cuhullin. But she didn't let on when he came back in.

OONA: Thank you kindly. There's just one other thing, I'm hoping you won't mind my asking.

CUHULLIN: Ask on, good woman.

OONA: Fin was going to make a new well for me near the house, but he forgot to do it, he left in such a terrible temper. There's water under all that rock for certain—all you need to do is pull the mountain apart.

CUHULLIN: All right, then, I'll see if I can find it for you.

NARRATOR 1: Off he went again. From the front door, Oona watched him put his big fingers into a little crack in the rock. And with a couple of tugs, he ripped open the mountainside so the water gushed out.

NARRATOR 4: Now, Oona had made up that one too, so when he came back, she again tried not to look surprised.

OONA: *(warmly)* Come in now and eat.

NARRATOR 2: She sat him down and put his food before him, with a big pile of bread loaves—the ones she'd made with the iron griddles inside.

CUHULLIN: Now, that's fine-looking bread.

NARRATOR 3: Cuhullin picked up a loaf and sunk his teeth into it.

CUHULLIN: *(bites down, then jumps up, roaring with pain)* Aaahhhhhh! A thousand thunderbolts! Woman, what did you put in your bread?!

OONA: *(acting surprised)* Nothing! What ails you, tall man? That's the bread my husband eats six dozen loaves of, every day!

CUHULLIN: *(dumbfounded)* You mean he eats this stuff?! Sure it is hard as rock, and I've lost one of me good front teeth on the first mouthful!

OONA: Didn't I say you were a poor, weak thing compared to Fin? Ach, you'll regret the day he gets his hands on *you*.

CUHULLIN: *(pulling himself up proudly)* Nonsense! If *he* can eat this bread, so can I!

NARRATOR 1: He picked up another loaf and dug his teeth into it.

CUHULLIN: *(bites down again, then roars with pain)* Aaahhhhhh! I've lost me other front tooth!

OONA: Man, it's a good job you never met up with Fin! It's more than your two front *teeth* you'd have lost.

CUHULLIN: You're tricking me! I don't believe *any* man eats bread like that!

OONA: Oh, don't you now! Just wait till you see *this*.

NARRATOR 4: She took one of the loaves off the table and walked over to the cradle where Fin was lying dressed like a baby.

OONA: This is Fin's *son*. Isn't he a fine little lad! *(tickles Fin under the chin)* Just like his daddy.

FIN: *(like a baby)* Goo, goo! Goo, goo!

OONA: *(to FIN, as to a baby, while holding out the loaf)* Here you are, me dove, have a bit of bread.

FIN: *(looks fearfully at the loaf, then questioningly at OONA)*

NARRATOR 2: Now, this loaf looked like all the rest, but Oona knew it was the only one *without* an iron griddle.

NARRATOR 3: She gave Fin a big wink. Then Fin took a bite of the loaf that took away half the side of it.

FIN: *(bites into the bread, then chews while making happy baby sounds)*

CUHULLIN: *(staring at FIN)* That's amazing! And you tell me this is Fin MacCool's child?

OONA: None other! So you can guess what size of man his *daddy* is.

CUHULLIN: *(still staring)* He must have a powerful set of teeth!

NARRATOR 1: Now, this was just what Oona was hoping for.

OONA: Oh, a *grand* set. Just slip your finger in there to feel them. *(to FIN)* Open your mouth now, baby, and let the nice man put in his big, strong finger. *(gives him another big wink)*

NARRATOR 4: So Cuhullin slipped his great right forefinger into Fin's mouth.

OONA: *(to CUHULLIN)* Push it well in, till you feel the back ones.

NARRATOR 2: Cuhullin pushed in his finger as far as it would go.

NARRATOR 3: Snap!—Fin bit it off, swallowed it, then leapt from the cradle.

FIN: *(whoops with delight)*

CUHULLIN: *(roars with pain and holds up his hand with the forefinger missing, staring at it in disbelief)*

FIN: *(throws off his nightgown, then speaks threateningly)* Now, what did you say you'd do to Fin MacCool?

CUHULLIN: *(stares and roars with anger at FIN)*

NARRATOR 1: Cuhullin made a great swipe at Fin with his fist.

CUHULLIN: *(hits FIN with his right hand, then wails with pain, holding his hand limply)*

NARRATOR 4: But he'd lost his finger, and all his strength with it, so all he did was hurt his hand.

CUHULLIN: *(roars in frustration, then turns and runs off)*

FIN: *(running off after him)* Ach, yes, you'd *better* run!

OONA: *(calling after Fin and smiling)* Now, Fin, don't be too hard on the poor thing!

NARRATOR 2: Fin chased Cuhullin halfway across Ireland before he let him go.

NARRATOR 3: And after that, he was free to get on with his road.

EXERCISE

The Giant's Wife: A Tale of Ireland is a fascinating piece of Irish folklore that blends imagination, humour, and cultural tradition. As a prominent 19th-century Irish writer, Carleton was well known for capturing the spirit of rural Ireland and preserving its oral tales. In this story, he weaves elements of myth and legend to create a lively narrative about giants, wit, and human nature. Rich in Irish cultural flavour, the tale not only entertains but also reflects the storytelling tradition through which values, beliefs, and humour were passed down generations. With its folk setting and larger-than-life characters, the story illustrates Carleton's unique ability to transform folklore into engaging literature.

I. Enumerate the traits of a strong, independent woman you admire who possesses the same power and strength as the giant's wife.

II. He or him is used as a generic term for a hypothetical individual. Instead, reframe your sentences in the plural. For example:
   - Each student should save **his** responses to the questions.
   - Students should save **their** responses to the questions.

III. Replace gender-linked titles with neutral titles. For Example:

Fireman	Firefighter
Policeman	Police officer
Chairman	Chairperson
Housewife	Homemaker

Pride

Dahlia Ravikovitch

Even rocks crack, I'm telling you,
and not on account of age.
For years they lie on their backs
in the heat and the cold,
so many years,
it almost creates the illusion of calm.
They don't move, so the cracks stay hidden.
A kind of pride.
Years pass over them as they wait.
Whoever is going to shatter them
hasn't come yet.
And so the moss flourishes, the seaweed
whips around,
the sea bursts forth and rolls back –
and still they seem motionless.
Till a little seal comes to rub up against the rocks,
comes and goes.
And suddenly the rock has an open wound.
I told you, when rocks crack, it comes as a surprise.
All the more so, people.

Exercise

Pride is a powerful poem that explores people who seem strong and unbreakable on the outside, like rocks, but deep inside carry hidden pain. The poem reminds us that even the toughest individuals can be vulnerable and hurt.

I. Write a personal reflection or fictional story about a moment when a word, gesture, or memory unexpectedly affected you or someone you know deeply.Focus on the contrast between external strength and inner vulnerability.

II. **Time travel with tenses**

(a) Imagine you are a time-traveling storyteller visiting the life of a rock. Fill in the blanks with the correct verb forms (past, present, or present perfect):

The rock ________ (lie) on the shore for hundreds of years. It ________ (feel) the sun, the storm, and the silence. But it never ________ (show) its pain. People ________ (walk) past it, thinking it was strong. One day, a seal ________ (come) close, and everything changed.

(b) **Preposition Maze – Find the Way**

The rock wants to tell its story, but its prepositions are missing!

I lie ________ my back, still and silent. Time moves ________ me, and the sea rushes ________. Moss grows ________ my sides. A seal brushes ________ me, and a crack opens ________ my heart.

III. Write your own 4-line poem that:

Has one **preposition**
Includes **a verb in the past tense**
Uses **an article**
Ends with a **pronoun**

New Words for New Years

Shashi Tharoor

Each year brings its share of infusions into the English language, and various publications end each year with the customary genuflections to various 'Words of the Year' anointed by assorted dictionaries. Some go further, and refuse to let January pass without looking ahead to possible words we'd need to use in the New Year. After all, before the Covid pandemic, whoever thought we would become so rapidly familiar with terms like 'herd immunity', 'social distancing', 'flatten the curve', 'viral load', 'spike protein', and 'mRNA vaccines'? Why wouldn't the same thing happen to us in future years that broadened our vocabularies from 2020 to 2022?

That venerable custodian of Anglophile wisdom, *The Economist* (which despite being weekly magazine, insists on calling itself a newspaper), in 2022 picked twenty-three terms it thought might catch on in the near future. Some of them are too technical, in this layman's opinion, to ever become the stuff of daily conversation- phrases like 'post-quantum cryptography' and 'cislunar', for instance. (The former would take too long to explain; the later relates to the space between Earth and the orbit of the Moon). Some others are too culturally specific to be applicable to most of us, even if those in *The Economist*'s orbit disagree- a term like

'TWaT cities', for instance, which in the US relate to cities where the working week has been reduced to Tuesdays, Wednesday, and Thursdays, with people working for home on Mondays and Fridays. But some of the others on *The Economist* list might well be words we will all need to master before the New Year is out.

Take 'synfuels', for example. These are synthetic fuels, produced artificially rather than being made from oil- highly relevant in an era where governments are more determined than ever to turn away from fossil fuels and look for renewable sources of energy. Or 'green hydrogen', hydrogen made using renewable energy through techniques that use electrolysis to split water into hydrogen and oxygen. This is both cheaper and less polluting than conventional fuel, and Western countries are already promoting the use of 'green hydrogen' as the best form of renewable energy.

Indeed, climate change and environmental consciousness may continue to have as great an impact on our vocabulary in the proximate future as Covid has had. We'll need to understand about 'Scope 1,2 and 3 emissions'; respectively, those caused directly caused by a company's activities (Scope 1), indirect emissions (Scope 2) and all other emissions that arise from the activities of a company's suppliers and customers (Scope 3). These three kinds of emissions are going to be part of discussions about responsibility for global warming. Higher temperatures caused by climate change are leading to 'aridification', or the long-term drying of a region or an area- another neologism. Similarly, responses to increasing heatwaves will add to our vocabulary-cities like Los Angeles, Phoenix, and Tokyo are planning measures to reduce temperatures by introducing 'cool roofs' (covered with white paint or reflective materials) and 'cool pavements' (sidewalks treated with special coatings) to reflect sunlight away so that surfaces absorb less heat. Some may create 'resilience hubs'- buildings that provide air-conditioned oases of refuge with drinking water, internet access, and phone-charging facilities- within cities to combat heatwaves.

If climate change will add to our list of regularly -used neologisms, technology will continue to intrude as well. One term is already widely in use: 'eSIMs' have begun to supplant or replace SIM cards, the subscriber identity modules we've been inserting into our phones to connect to different networks. 'eSIMs' have begun to replace physical chips with digital codes that are part of the software on your phone.

Thanks to technology, 'reality' is already undergoing dizzying change. We already have 'virtual reality', when you wear a pair of goggles and a headset that immerse you in an alternative, computer-generated reality. Next there will be 'augmented reality', which will superimpose computer-generated elements onto your view of the real world. Watch out for 'mixed reality', which will go even farther by allowing real and virtual items to interact. What is real and what is digitally-generated will blend into each other in ways that may easily affect our vocabulary, our daily lives and one day, our sanity!

Exercise

Shashi Tharoor introduces some unique and thoughtful words that capture emotions and ideas we often struggle to express. Words like "omnivestitude" (feeling deeply connected to the universe), "atmaami" (a soul-level bond), and "aeternamour" (love that lasts forever) invite us to start the year with fresh energy and deeper meaning. With his usual love for language, Tharoor encourages us to think beyond the ordinary and embrace the power of words to inspire change and connection.

I. Write a few Positive and Empowering resolutions for a new year with the words given below:

For Example:

1. Renewal — A fresh start, new beginnings.
2. Intention — Focused and purposeful goals.
3. Gratitude — Thankfulness for what we have.
4. Resilience — Bouncing back from challenges.
5. Harmony — Balance and peace in life.
6. Growth — Personal, emotional, or spiritual development.
7. Abundance — More of what you seek (love, success, joy).
8. Courage — Strength to take risks and try new things.
9. Mindfulness — Living in the present moment.
10. Joyfulness — Choosing happiness in little things.

II.

(a) **Vocabulary: "Welcoming the New Year with Rejuvenating Words"**

Match the word with its meaning:

1. Resilience
2. Intention
3. Abundance
4. Renewal
5. Gratitude

Meanings:

A. A feeling of thankfulness and appreciation
B. A fresh start or beginning again
C. The ability to recover from difficulties
D. Having more than enough of something
E. A clear purpose or plan

(b) **Fill in the Blanks by using the given words:**
Words: courage, harmony, joy, purpose, hope

1. I start this New Year with a sense of ________ for better days ahead.
2. Helping others brings me great ________.
3. When I follow my ________, I feel more fulfilled.
4. Let's live in ________ with others and with nature.
5. It takes ________ to make meaningful change.

(c) Choose any two words from the list below and write a short paragraph (5–7 lines) about your hopes for the New Year using both words meaningfully.

Words: Transformation – Mindfulness – Empower – Vision – Perseverance – Joyfulness

III. Word Scramble – Unscramble these positive words:

1. gloe → ________
2. rjoyuens → ________
3. cuesoss → ________
4. wghotr → ________
5. encidnefoc → ______

Angels and Blueberries

Tara Campbell

"Why is the sky blue?" you ask.

Well, it all depends on who's answering.

If you ask a grown-up, you'll probably get an answer about light, and how it bounces off air particles, and how certain wavelengths (i.e. colors) get absorbed, and certain colors (i.e. wavelengths) get kicked back out, and those certain colors/wavelengths (i.e. blue) are the ones that you and I can see.

If you ask a scientist, you'll likely get an even more confusing but way more convincing version of that answer.

But if you ask a writer, you'll get a different answer every time.

One answer, for example, lies with the special properties of blue fingerpaint. Whenever children use blue paint, tiny particles of it dissolve from their hands into the air and colour it blue. Over time the pigment fades, but as long as there is fingerpainting, there will always be blue sky.

Another answer is related to the blue-eyed creatures at the North and South Poles. They are always looking up into the sky, and the blue of their eyes reflects back for the whole world to see. You've probably never heard of these polar creatures because they know how to hide from satellites and explorers. The reflection of their eyes is all we'll ever see of them.

But the answer I think is true right now concerns angels and blueberries.

You see, blueberries are the angels' favourite food. There's nothing they like more; and berries are healthy, so it's a happy coincidence. The only problem is, angels are sloppy eaters, and they eat pretty much all day. Of course, they do other things like play the harp and sing and keep little babies from getting into the bleach under the sink. But they still have lots of time to munch on blueberries—they live forever, after all—so little bits of blueberry wind up all over the sky.

Even worse, some angels don't like the blueberry skins, so they peel each berry before eating it and toss the skins to the side. This doesn't make them blatant litterers, mind you—they know they'll get around to picking up the skins, just not at that very moment.

So as the day goes on, the angels eat more and more berries; and as the sun goes down, its light reflects through the berry pulp and juice, creating wonderful reds and oranges and yellows. And still the angels eat, and the sky grows darker and darker with blue skins and bits of berry. The angels keep on munching until, with the exception of little gaps for the moon and stars, no light can get to the Earth at all. In fact, there's not even enough room for the moon most of the time, which is why you only see the whole thing once a month.

In the middle of the night God finally has enough, and she tells the angels they have to start cleaning up their mess. Of course they start right away, but it's a big mess and it takes a while. And as they clean, you can see a little bit of light start to penetrate the layer of blueberry waste. Dawn begins as they wipe and scrub, and daylight breaks when they finally clear away enough blueberries for the sun to shine on the Earth again.

The one problem is that blueberry skins stain, and the angels can't scrub the traces away completely. Some days they do better, and the sky is light blue. But on very sunny days you can see the full extent of the staining and the sky is a rich, dark blue. But God isn't that concerned about the stains. She actually thinks they're pretty, and the renters down on the surface don't mind, and she's not planning on moving anytime soon, so it's not like she has to worry about resale value. What matters to her is that the angels did their best.

Now, you may wonder what would happen if the angels ever got tired of blueberries. What would happen if they switched to raspberries? Would the sky eventually wind up purple? If they started eating bananas, would the yellow peels turn the blue sky green? Or if they developed a fondness for lemons, would the juice bleach the colour out forever? And if that happened, would your grandchildren ever believe the sky had once been blue?

Or would they just think you were a silly writer telling stories about angels and blueberries?

Exercise

Angels and Blueberries is a playful piece of flash fiction that offers a magical take on a common question: "Why is the sky blue?" Instead of turning to science, Campbell crafts a delightful explanation—angels, while eating blueberries, accidentally stain the sky with juice as they peel and enjoy the fruit. These celestial beings are portrayed as lovable yet clumsy, leaving behind a bluish sky that lingers until morning, when a few angels try to clean up—but not thoroughly.

Blending humour with imagination, the story transforms simple, everyday elements—like angels and fruit—into a vivid and enchanting metaphor. It encourages readers to see the world through a more creative and whimsical lens, highlighting how even the shortest stories can inspire wonder and reinterpret the ordinary in extraordinary ways. This piece is a charming example of how metaphor and fantasy can enrich storytelling and spark imaginative thinking.

I. "Explain a natural phenomenon with a whimsical tale:
   (a) what if elves painted rainbows (or)
   (b) Stars were tiny lantern insects?

   Follow the structure:

   - Begin with a question – "Why…?"

- Offer alternative, playful causes.
- Introduce a turning point.
- Conclude with reflective questions or a twist.

II. Micro Fiction:
Write a micro fiction of 100 words based on a "natural mystery" (e.g., why rain falls? why the wind sings? why the sun rises?). Focus on brevity, surprise, word economy, and sustaining a playful tone.

III. Write about your earliest memory of playing a favourite game with your friend or about your favourite teacher in school?

Dreams

Langston Hughes

Hold fast to dreams
For if dreams die
Life is a broken-winged bird
That cannot fly.

Hold fast to dreams
For when dreams go
Life is a barren field
Frozen with snow.

Exercise

Langston Hughes' Dreams tells us to always hold on to our dreams because without them, life becomes empty and hopeless. He compares a dreamless life to a broken-winged bird that can't fly and a barren, frozen field—showing that dreams give life purpose and joy.

I. Multiple Choice Questions

1. What is the core message expressed in the poem *Dreams*?

(a) Dreams are only for the young
(b) Dreams are unimportant
(c) Dreams give life purpose
(d) Dreams are dangerous

2. Which idea is symbolized by the phrase "Life is a broken-winged bird" in the poem *Dreams*?
   (a) Life is full of hope
   (b) Birds are unlucky symbols in poetry
   (c) A dreamless life is like a bird with no wing
   (d) Nature is more powerful than human effort
3. What does the speaker urge the reader to do in the poem *Dreams* by Langston Hughes?
   (a) Forget their dreams and live in the moment.
   (b) Work hard without thinking about dreams.
   (c) Hold fast to their dreams and never let them go.
   (d) Wait for dreams to come true on their own
4. According to the poem *Dreams*, how is life affected when dreams die?
   (a) Life becomes joyful and carefree.
   (b) Life turns empty and without purpose.
   (c) Life becomes like a bird that cannot fly.
   (d) Life continues normally without any change.

II. Write a short reflective note on your personal dreams and the progress you have made toward achieving them.

III. Prepare a motivational speech on Pursuing one's dream to aim high in life.

Letters from a Father to His Daughter

Jawaharlal Nehru

Language, Writing and Numerals

We have already considered the various languages and how they are related to each other. Let us think for a while how language must have begun. We find among some animals that there are some words used. The monkeys, it is said, have a few cries or words for simple things. You can also notice the peculiar cries that some animals make when they are frightened and want to warn others of their kind of danger.

Perhaps language started in the same way in man. There must have been very simple cries to begin with—cries of fear and warning. Then, it may be, came what are called labour cries. When a number of people work together they usually make a noise together. Have you not noticed people pulling together at something? Or lifting a great weight together? It seems that all crying together helps them a little. These labour cries might have been the first words that man used.

Gradually other words must have come in—simple words like water, fire, horse, and bear. Probably there were only nouns and no verbs. If a man wanted to say that he had seen a bear he would only say one word "bear" and point, just like a child. There could hardly be much conversation then!

Language developed. Short sentences came and longer ones. Probably there was not one language for all the different people at any time. But at some time there could not have been very many different languages. As I have already told you, there were a few languages then, each of which developed a large family of languages.

During the time of the early civilisations, which we have been considering, language had already greatly developed. There were many songs, and bards and singers used to sing them. There was not much writing or books in those days and so people had to remember much more. It is easier to remember rhymes and poetry. Therefore we find that rhymes and ballads were very popular in all these countries where the early civilisations existed.

The singers or bards were specially fond of singing of the glories of dead heroes. People in those days were most interested in fighting and so the songs are about bravery in battle. We find this in India as well as in other countries.

Writing also has had an interesting beginning. I have referred to Chinese writing. All writing must have begun with pictures. A man who wanted to say something about a peacock would try to make a picture or drawing of a peacock. Of course no one could write much this way. Gradually the pictures would have become simpler and simpler. Much later an alphabet was thought of and evolved. This immediately made writing far easier and progress became more rapid.

Numerals and counting must have been a great discovery. Without numerals it is difficult to imagine how any kind of business could be done. The person who invented numerals must have been a genius or a very clever person. At first in Europe numerals were rather clumsy. You know what are called the Roman numerals —I, II, III, IV, V, VI, VII, VIII, IX, X and so on. These are clumsy and difficult to manage. The numerals we use now, in all languages, are very much better. I refer to I, 2, 3, 4, 5, 6 , 7, 8, 9, 10. These are called Arabic numerals because people in Europe got to know them through the Arabs. But the Arabs themselves learnt them from the Indians, so it would be more correct to call them Indian numerals.

But I am going too fast. We have not come to the Arabs yet.

Exercise

'Letters to Indira' is a collection of letters written by Jawaharlal Nehru to his daughter Indira during his imprisonment in the 1930s. These letters cover a wide range of topics, including history, culture, and politics, as Nehru aimed to educate Indira about the world and its complexities. This letter, 'Language, Writing and Numerals,' explores the origins of human communication and how it evolved over time.

I. The origin of language stretches back to the dawn of human history and continues to shape the way we communicate today. To understand the evolution of language, it is important to trace back to the primitive sounds that formed the modern words.

Try to find five modern words that originated from primitive sounds.

1. ______________________________
2. ______________________________
3. ______________________________
4. ______________________________
5. ______________________________

II. The English Language has many borrowed words from other languages. Identify some loanwords that are used in daily communication.

III. Draft a letter to your parents about your dreams and goals in life.

Why I Write

George Orwell

From a very early age, perhaps the age of five or six, I knew that when I grew up I should be a writer. Between the ages of about seventeen and twenty-four I tried to abandon this idea, but I did so with the consciousness that I was outraging my true nature and that sooner or later I should have to settle down and write books.

I was the middle child of three, but there was a gap of five years on either side, and I barely saw my father before I was eight. For this and other reasons I was somewhat lonely, and I soon developed disagreeable mannerisms which made me unpopular throughout my schooldays. I had the lonely child's habit of making up stories and holding conversations with imaginary persons, and I think from the very start my literary ambitions were mixed up with the feeling of being isolated and undervalued. I knew that I had a facility with words and a power of facing unpleasant facts, and I felt that this created a sort of private world in which I could get my own back for my failure in everyday life. Nevertheless the volume of serious—i.e. seriously intended—writing which I produced all through my childhood and boyhood would not amount to half a dozen pages. I wrote my first poem at the age of four or five, my mother taking it down to dictation. I cannot remember anything about it except that it was about a tiger and the tiger had 'chair-like teeth' — a good enough phrase, but I fancy the poem was a plagiarism of Blake's 'Tiger, Tiger'. At eleven, when the war or 1914-18 broke out, I wrote a patriotic poem which was printed in the local newspaper, as was another, two years later, on the death of Kitchener. From time to time, when I was a bit older, I wrote bad and usually unfinished 'nature poems' in the Georgian style. I also attempted a short story which was a ghastly failure. That was the total of the would-be serious work that I actually set down on paper during all those years.

However, throughout this time I did in a sense engage in literary activities. To begin with there was the made-to-order stuff which I produced quickly, easily and without much pleasure to myself. Apart from school work, I wrote *vers d'occasion*, semi-comic poems which I could turn out at what now seems to me astonishing speed—at fourteen I wrote a whole rhyming play, in imitation of Aristophanes, in about a week—and helped to edit a school magazines, both printed and in manuscript. These magazines were the most pitiful burlesque stuff that you could imagine, and I took far less trouble with them than I now would with the cheapest journalism. But side by side with all this, for fifteen years or more, I was carrying out a literary exercise of a quite different kind: this was the making up of a continuous 'story' about myself, a sort of diary existing only in the mind. I believe this is a common habit of children and adolescents. As a very small child I used to imagine that I was, say, Robin Hood, and picture myself as the hero of thrilling adventures, but quite soon my 'story' ceased to be narcissistic in a crude way and became more and more a mere description of what I was doing and the things I saw. For minutes at a time this kind of thing would be running through my head: 'He pushed the door open and entered the room. A yellow beam of sunlight, filtering through the muslin curtains, slanted on to the table, where a match-box, half-open, lay beside the inkpot. With his right hand in his pocket he moved across to the window. Down in the street a tortoiseshell cat was chasing a dead leaf', etc. This habit continued until I was about twenty-five, right through my non-literary years. Although I had to search, and did search, for the right words, I seemed to be making this descriptive effort almost against my will, under a kind of compulsion from outside. The 'story' must, I suppose, have reflected the styles of the various writers I admired at different ages, but so far as I remember it always had the same meticulous descriptive quality.

When I was about sixteen I suddenly discovered the joy of mere words, i.e. the sounds and associations of words. The lines from *Paradise Lost*—

> So hee with difficulty and labour hard
> Moved on: with difficulty and labour hee.

which do not now seem to me so very wonderful, sent shivers down my backbone; and the spelling 'hee' for 'he' was an added pleasure. As for the need to describe things, I knew all about it already. So it is clear what kind of books I wanted to write, in so far as I could be said to want to write books at that time. I wanted to write enormous naturalistic novels with unhappy endings, full of detailed descriptions and arresting similes, and also full of purple passages in which words were used partly for the sake of their own sound. And in fact my first completed novel, *Burmese Days*, which I wrote when I was thirty but projected much earlier, is rather that kind of book.

I give all this background information because I do not think one can assess a writer's motives without knowing something of his early development. His subject matter will be determined by the age he lives in—at least this is true in tumultuous, revolutionary ages like our own—but before he ever begins to write he will have acquired an emotional attitude from which he will never completely escape. It is his job, no doubt, to discipline his temperament and avoid getting stuck at some immature stage, in some perverse mood; but if he escapes from his early influences altogether, he will have killed his impulse to write. Putting aside the need to earn a living, I think there are four great motives for writing, at any rate for writing prose. They exist in different degrees in every writer, and in any one writer the proportions will vary from time to time, according to the atmosphere in which he is living. They are:

(i) *Sheer egoism.* Desire to seem clever, to be talked about, to be remembered after death, to get your own back on the grown-ups who snubbed you in childhood, etc. It is humbug to pretend this is not a motive, and a strong one. Writers share this characteristic with scientists, artists, politicians, lawyers, soldiers, successful businessmen—in short, with the whole top crust of humanity. The great mass of human beings are not acutely selfish. After the age of about thirty they almost abandon the sense of being individuals at all — and live chiefly for others, or are simply smothered under drudgery. But there is also the minority of gifted, willful people who are determined to live their own lives to the end, and writers belong in this class. Serious writers, I should say, are on the whole more vain and self-centered than journalists, though less interested in money.

(ii) *Aesthetic enthusiasm.* Perception of beauty in the external world, or, on the other hand, in words and their right arrangement. Pleasure in the impact of one sound on another, in the firmness of good prose or the rhythm of a good story. Desire to share an experience which one feels is valuable and ought not to be missed. The aesthetic motive is very feeble in a lot of writers, but even a pamphleteer or writer of textbooks will have pet words and phrases which appeal to him for non-utilitarian reasons; or he may feel strongly about typography, width of margins, etc. Above the level of a railway guide, no book is quite free from aesthetic considerations.

(iii) *Historical impulse.* Desire to see things as they are, to find out true facts and store them up for the use of posterity.

(iv) *Political purpose.* Using the word 'political' in the widest possible sense. Desire to push the world in a certain direction, to alter other peoples' idea of the kind of society that they should strive after. Once again, no book is genuinely free from political bias. The opinion that art should have nothing to do with politics is itself a political attitude.

It can be seen how these various impulses must war against one another, and how they must fluctuate from person to person and from time to time. By nature — taking your 'nature' to be the state you have attained when you are first adult — I am a person in whom the first three motives would outweigh the fourth. In a peaceful age I might have written ornate or merely descriptive books, and might have remained almost unaware of my political loyalties. As it is I have been forced into becoming a sort of pamphleteer. First I spent five years in an unsuitable profession (the Indian Imperial Police, in Burma), and then I underwent poverty and the sense of failure. This increased my natural hatred of authority and made me for the first time fully aware of the existence of the working classes, and the job in Burma had given me some understanding of the nature of imperialism: but these experiences were not enough to give me an accurate political orientation. Then came Hitler, the Spanish Civil War, etc. By the end of 1935 I had still failed to reach a firm decision. I remember a little poem that I wrote at that date, expressing my dilemma:

A happy vicar I might have been
Two hundred years ago
To preach upon eternal doom
And watch my walnuts grow;

But born, alas, in an evil time,
I missed that pleasant haven,
For the hair has grown on my upper lip
And the clergy are all clean-shaven.

And later still the times were good,
We were so easy to please,
We rocked our troubled thoughts to sleep
On the bosoms of the trees.

All ignorant we dared to own
The joys we now dissemble;
The greenfinch on the apple bough
Could make my enemies tremble.

But girl's bellies and apricots,
Roach in a shaded stream,
Horses, ducks in flight at dawn,
All these are a dream.

It is forbidden to dream again;
We maim our joys or hide them:
Horses are made of chromium steel
And little fat men shall ride them.

I am the worm who never turned,
The eunuch without a harem;
Between the priest and the commissar
I walk like Eugene Aram;

And the commissar is telling my fortune
While the radio plays,
But the priest has promised an Austin Seven,
For Duggie always pays.

I dreamt I dwelt in marble halls,
And woke to find it true;
I wasn't born for an age like this;
Was Smith? Was Jones? Were you?

The Spanish war and other events in 1936-37 turned the scale and thereafter I knew where I stood. Every line of serious work that I have written since 1936 has been written, directly or indirectly, *against* totalitarianism and *for* democratic socialism, as I understand it. It seems to me nonsense, in a period like our own, to think that one can avoid writing of such subjects. Everyone writes of them in one guise or another. It is simply a question of which side one takes and what approach one follows. And the more one is conscious of one›s political bias, the more chance one has of acting politically without sacrificing one›s aesthetic and intellectual integrity.

What I have most wanted to do throughout the past ten years is to make political writing into an art. My starting point is always a feeling of partisanship, a sense of injustice. When I sit down to write a book, I do not say to myself, 'I am going to produce a work of art'. I write it because there is some lie that I want to expose, some fact to which I want to draw attention, and my initial concern is to get a hearing. But I could not do the work of writing a book, or even a long magazine article, if it were not also an aesthetic experience. Anyone who cares to examine my work will see that even when it is downright propaganda it contains much that a full-time politician would consider irrelevant. I am not able, and do not want, completely to abandon the world view that I acquired in childhood. So long as I remain alive and well I shall continue to feel strongly about prose style, to love the surface of the earth, and to take a pleasure in solid objects and scraps of useless information. It is no use trying to suppress that side of myself. The job is to reconcile my ingrained likes and dislikes with the essentially public, non-individual activities that this age forces on all of us.

It is not easy. It raises problems of construction and of language, and it raises in a new way the problem of truthfulness. Let me give just one example of the cruder kind of difficulty that arises. My book about the Spanish civil war, *Homage to Catalonia*, is of course a frankly political book, but in the main it is written with a certain detachment and regard for form. I did try very hard in it to tell the whole truth without violating my literary instincts. But among other things it contains a long chapter, full of newspaper quotations and the like, defending the Trotskyists who were accused of plotting with Franco. Clearly such a chapter, which after a year or two would lose its interest for any ordinary reader, must ruin the book. A critic whom I respect read me a lecture about it. 'Why did you put in all that stuff?' he said. 'You've turned what might have been a good book into journalism.' What he said was true, but I could not have done otherwise. I happened to know, what very few people in England had been allowed to know, that innocent men were being falsely accused. If I had not been angry about that I should never have written the book.

In one form or another this problem comes up again. The problem of language is subtler and would take too long to discuss. I will only say that of late years I have tried to write less picturesquely and more exactly. In any case I find that by the time you have perfected any style of writing, you have always outgrown it. *Animal Farm* was the first book in which I tried, with full consciousness of what I was doing, to fuse political purpose and artistic purpose into one whole. I have not written a novel for seven years, but I hope to write another fairly soon. It is bound to be a failure, every book is a failure, but I do know with some clarity what kind of book I want to write.

Looking back through the last page or two, I see that I have made it appear as though my motives in writing were wholly public-spirited. I don't want to leave that as the final impression. All writers are vain, selfish, and lazy, and at the very bottom of their motives there lies a mystery. Writing a book is a horrible, exhausting struggle, like a long bout of some painful illness. One would never undertake such a thing if one were not driven on by some demon whom one can neither resist nor understand. For all one knows that demon is simply the same instinct that makes a baby squall for attention. And yet it is also true that one can write nothing readable unless one constantly struggles to efface one's own personality. Good prose is like a windowpane. I cannot say with certainty which of my motives are the strongest, but I know which of them deserve to be followed. And looking back through my work, I see that it is invariably where I lacked a political purpose that I wrote lifeless books and was betrayed into purple passages, sentences without meaning, decorative adjectives and humbug generally.

1946

Exercise

In this autobiographical essay, George Orwell explains the reasons behind his decision to become a writer. He reflects on his childhood, the political events that shaped his thinking, and his desire to expose lies and defend truth. Orwell identifies four motives for writing: sheer egoism, aesthetic enthusiasm, historical impulse, and political purpose. The essay gives insight into the connection between politics and literature in Orwell's work.

I. Diary to Prose

Orwell describes how, as a boy, he would narrate daily life in a highly descriptive, story-like way. Try this yourself — take a simple, everyday moment from your morning and turn it into a short, descriptive prose passage in Orwell's style.

For Example: Original moment: I drank tea and looked out of the window.

Prose version: He lifted the steaming cup to his lips, the faint scent of ginger and cardamom drifting upwards. Beyond the glass, a grey morning settled over the street, the pavement still slick from last night's rain. A lone crow flapped lazily to the crooked branch of the neem tree, its wings black against the washed-out sky.

II. Quote to Poster

Pick one striking quote from Orwell's Why I Write and design a poster that captures the essence of that quote.

III. Write a note of appreciation of a poem, story or a play which you enjoyed reading.

Kabuliwala

Rabindranath Tagore

My five years' old daughter Mini cannot live without chattering. I really believe that in all her life she has not wasted a minute in silence. Her mother is often vexed at this, and would stop her prattle, but I would not. To see Mini quiet is unnatural, and I cannot bear it long. And so my own talk with her is always lively.

One morning, for instance, when I was in the midst of the seventeenth chapter of my new novel, my little Mini stole into the room, and putting her hand into mine, said: "Father! Ramdayal the doorkeeper calls a crow a krow! He doesn't know anything, does he?"

Before I could explain to her the differences of language in this world, she was embarked on the full tide of another subject. "What do you think, Father? Bhola says there is an elephant in the clouds, blowing water out of his trunk, and that is why it rains!"

And then, darting off anew, while I sat still making ready some reply to this last saying, "Father! what relation is Mother to you?"

"My dear little sister in the law!" I murmured involuntarily to myself, but with a grave face contrived to answer: "Go and play with Bhola, Mini! I am busy!"

The window of my room overlooks the road. The child had seated herself at my feet near my table, and was playing softly, drumming on her knees. I was hard at work on my seventeenth chapter, where Protrap Singh, the hero, had just caught Kanchanlata, the heroine, in his arms, and was about to escape with her by the third story window of the castle, when all of a sudden Mini left her play, and ran to the window, crying, "A Kabuliwallah! a Kabuliwallah!" Sure enough in the street below was a Kabuliwallah, passing slowly along. He wore the loose soiled clothing of his people, with a tall turban; there was a bag on his back, and he carried boxes of grapes in his hand.

I cannot tell what were my daughter's feelings at the sight of this man, but she began to call him loudly. "Ah!" I thought, "he will come in, and my seventeenth chapter will never be finished!" At which exact moment the Kabuliwallah turned, and looked up at the child. When she saw this, overcome by terror, she fled to her mother's protection, and disappeared. She had a blind belief that inside the bag, which the big man carried, there were perhaps two or three other children like herself. The pedlar meanwhile entered my doorway, and greeted me with a smiling face.

So precarious was the position of my hero and my heroine, that my first impulse was to stop and buy something, since the man had been called. I made some small purchases, and a conversation began about Abdurrahman, the Russians, the English, and the Frontier Policy.

As he was about to leave, he asked: "And where is the little girl, sir?"

And I, thinking that Mini must get rid of her false fear, had her brought out.

She stood by my chair, and looked at the Kabuliwallah and his bag. He offered her nuts and raisins, but she would not be tempted, and only clung the closer to me, with all her doubts increased.

This was their first meeting.

One morning, however, not many days later, as I was leaving the house, I was startled to find Mini, seated on a bench near the door, laughing and talking, with the great Kabuliwallah at her feet. In all her life, it appeared; my small daughter had never found so patient a listener, save her father. And already the corner of her little sari was stuffed with almonds and raisins, the gift of her visitor, "Why did you give her those?" I said, and taking out an eight-anna bit, I handed it to him. The man accepted the money without demur, and slipped it into his pocket.

Alas, on my return an hour later, I found the unfortunate coin had made twice its own worth of trouble! For the Kabuliwallah had given it to Mini, and her mother catching sight of the bright round object, had pounced on the child with: "Where did you get that eight-anna bit? "

"The Kabuliwallah gave it me," said Mini cheerfully.

"The Kabuliwallah gave it you!" cried her mother much shocked. "Oh, Mini! how could you take it from him?"

I, entering at the moment, saved her from impending disaster, and proceeded to make my own inquiries.

It was not the first or second time, I found, that the two had met. The Kabuliwallah had overcome the child's first terror by a judicious bribery of nuts and almonds, and the two were now great friends.

They had many quaint jokes, which afforded them much amusement. Seated in front of him, looking down on his gigantic frame in all her tiny dignity, Mini would ripple her face with laughter, and begin: "O Kabuliwallah, Kabuliwallah, what have you got in your bag?"

And he would reply, in the nasal accents of the mountaineer: "An elephant!" Not much cause for merriment, perhaps; but how they both enjoyed the witticism! And for me, this child's talk with a grown-up man had always in it something strangely fascinating.

Then the Kabuliwallah, not to be behindhand, would take his turn: "Well, little one, and when are you going to the father-in-law's house?"

Now most small Bengali maidens have heard long ago about the father-in-law's house; but we, being a little new-fangled, had kept these things from our child, and Mini at this question must have been a trifle bewildered. But she would not show it, and with ready tact replied: "Are you going there?"

Amongst men of the Kabuliwallah's class, however, it is well known that the words father-in-law's house have a double meaning. It is a euphemism for jail, the place where we are well cared for, at no expense to ourselves. In this sense would the sturdy pedlar take my daughter's question. "Ah," he would say, shaking his fist at an invisible policeman, "I will thrash my father-in-law!" Hearing this, and picturing the poor discomfited relative, Mini would go off into peals of laughter, in which her formidable friend would join.

These were autumn mornings, the very time of year when kings of old went forth to conquest; and I, never stirring from my little corner in Calcutta, would let my mind wander over the whole world. At the very name of another country, my heart would go out to it, and at the sight of a foreigner in the streets, I would fall to weaving a network of dreams, --the mountains, the glens, and the forests of his distant home, with his cottage in its setting, and the free and independent life of far-away wilds.

Perhaps the scenes of travel conjure themselves up before me, and pass and repass in my imagination all the more vividly, because I lead such a vegetable existence, that a call to travel would fall upon me like a thunderbolt.

In the presence of this Kabuliwallah, I was immediately transported to the foot of arid mountain peaks, with narrow little defiles twisting in and out amongst their towering heights. I could see the string of camels bearing the merchandise, and the company of turbaned merchants, carrying some of their queer old firearms, and some of their spears, journeying downward towards the plains. I could see--but at some such point Mini's mother would intervene, imploring me to "beware of that man."

Mini's mother is unfortunately a very timid lady. Whenever she hears a noise in the street, or sees people coming towards the house, she always jumps to the conclusion that they are either thieves, or drunkards, or snakes, or tigers, or malaria or cockroaches, or caterpillars, or an English sailor. Even after all these years of experience, she is not able to overcome her terror. So she was full of doubts about the Kabuliwallah, and used to beg me to keep a watchful eye on him.

I tried to laugh her fear gently away, but then she would turn round on me seriously, and ask me solemn questions.

Were children never kidnapped?

Was it, then, not true that there was slavery in Kabul?

Was it so very absurd that this big man should be able to carry off a tiny child?

I urged that, though not impossible, it was highly improbable. But this was not enough, and her dread persisted. As it was indefinite, however, it did not seem right to forbid the man the house, and the intimacy went on unchecked.

Once a year in the middle of January Rahmun, the Kabuliwallah, was in the habit of returning to his country, and as the time approached he would be very busy, going from house to house collecting his debts. This year, however, he could always find time to come and see Mini. It would have seemed to an outsider that there was some conspiracy between the two, for when he could not come in the morning, he would appear in the evening.

Even to me it was a little startling now and then, in the corner of a dark room, suddenly to surprise this tall, loose-garmented, much bebagged man; but when Mini would run in smiling, with her, "O! Kabuliwallah! Kabuliwallah!" and the two friends, so far apart in age, would subside into their old laughter and their old jokes, I felt reassured.

One morning, a few days before he had made up his mind to go, I was correcting my proof sheets in my study. It was chilly weather. Through the window the rays of the sun touched my feet, and the slight warmth was very welcome. It was almost eight o'clock, and the early pedestrians were returning home, with their heads covered. All at once, I heard an uproar in the street, and, looking out, saw Rahmun being led away bound between two policemen, and behind them a crowd of curious boys. There were blood-stains on the clothes of the Kabuliwallah, and one of the policemen carried a knife.

Hurrying out, I stopped them, and enquired what it all meant. Partly from one, partly from another, I gathered that a certain neighbour had owed the pedlar something for a Rampuri shawl, but had falsely denied having bought it, and that in the course of the quarrel, Rahmun had struck him. Now in the heat of his excitement, the prisoner began calling his enemy all sorts of names, when suddenly in a verandah of my house appeared my little Mini, with her usual exclamation: "O Kabuliwallah! Kabuliwallah!" Rahmun's face lighted up as he turned to her. He had no bag under his arm today, so she could not discuss the elephant with him. She at once therefore proceeded to the next question: "Are you going to the father-in-law's house?" Rahmun laughed and said: "Just where I am going, little one!" Then seeing that the reply did not amuse the child, he held up his fettered hands. " Ali," he said, " I would have thrashed that old father-in-law, but my hands are bound!"

On a charge of murderous assault, Rahmun was sentenced to some years' imprisonment.

Time passed away, and he was not remembered. The accustomed work in the accustomed place was ours, and the thought of the once-free mountaineer spending his years in prison seldom or never occurred to us. Even my light-hearted Mini, I am ashamed to say, forgot her old friend. New companions filled her life. As she grew older, she spent more of her time with girls. So much time indeed did she spend with them that she came no more, as she used to do, to her father's room. I was scarcely on speaking terms with her.

Years had passed away. It was once more autumn and we had made arrangements for our Mini's marriage. It was to take place during the Puja Holidays. With Durga returning to Kailas, the light of our home also was to depart to her husband's house, and leave her father's in the shadow.

The morning was bright. After the rains, there was a sense of ablution in the air, and the sun-rays looked like pure gold. So bright were they that they gave a beautiful radiance even to the sordid brick walls of our Calcutta lanes. Since early dawn to-day the wedding-pipes had been sounding, and at each beat my own heart throbbed. The wail of the tune, Bhairavi, seemed to intensify my pain at the approaching separation. My Mini was to be married to-night.

From early morning noise and bustle had pervaded the house. In the courtyard the canopy had to be slung on its bamboo poles;

the chandeliers with their tinkling sound must be hung in each room and verandah. There was no end of hurry and excitement. I was sitting in my study, looking through the accounts, when some one entered, saluting respectfully, and stood before me. It was Rahmun the Kabuliwallah. At first I did not recognise him. He had no bag, nor the long hair, nor the same vigour that he used to have. But he smiled, and I knew him again.

"When did you come, Rahmun?" I asked him.

"Last evening," he said, "I was released from jail."

The words struck harsh upon my ears. I had never before talked with one who had wounded his fellow, and my heart shrank within itself, when I realised this, for I felt that the day would have been better-omened had he not turned up.

"There are ceremonies going on," I said, "and I am busy. Could you perhaps come another day?"

At once he turned to go; but as he reached the door he hesitated, and said: "May I not see the little one, sir, for a moment?" It was his belief that Mini was still the same. He had pictured her running to him as she used, calling "O Kabuliwallah! Kabuliwallah!" He had imagined too that they would laugh and talk together, just as of old. In fact, in memory of former days he had brought, carefully wrapped up in paper, a few almonds and raisins and grapes, obtained somehow from a countryman, for his own little fund was dispersed.

I said again: "There is a ceremony in the house, and you will not be able to see any one to-day."

The man's face fell. He looked wistfully at me for a moment, said "Good morning," and went out. I felt a little sorry, and would have called him back, but I found he was returning of his own accord. He came close up to me holding out his offerings and said: "I brought these few things, sir, for the little one. Will you give them to her?"

I took them and was going to pay him, but he caught my hand and said: "You are very kind, sir! Keep me in your recollection. Do not offer me money!--You have a little girl, I too have one like her in my own home. I think of her, and bring fruits to your child, not to make a profit for myself."

Saying this, he put his hand inside his big loose robe, and brought out a small and dirty piece of paper. With great care he unfolded this, and smoothed it out with both hands on my table. It bore the impression of a little band. Not a photograph. Not a drawing. The impression of an ink-smeared hand laid flat on the paper. This touch of his own little daughter had been always on his heart, as he had come year after year to Calcutta, to sell his wares in the streets.

Tears came to my eyes. I forgot that he was a poor Kabuli fruit-seller, while I was--but no, what was I more than he? He also was a father. That impression of the hand of his little Parbati in her distant mountain home reminded me of my own little Mini.

I sent for Mini immediately from the inner apartment. Many difficulties were raised, but I would not listen. Clad in the red silk of her wedding-day, with the sandal paste on her forehead, and adorned as a young bride, Mini came, and stood bashfully before me.

The Kabuliwallah looked a little staggered at the apparition. He could not revive their old friendship. At last he smiled and said: "Little one, are you going to your father-in-law's house?"

But Mini now understood the meaning of the word "father-in-law," and she could not reply to him as of old. She flushed up at the question, and stood before him with her bride-like face turned down.

I remembered the day when the Kabuliwallah and my Mini had first met, and I felt sad. When she had gone, Rahmun heaved a deep sigh, and sat down on the floor. The idea had suddenly come to him that his daughter too must have grown in this long time, and that he would have to make friends with her anew. Assuredly he would not find her, as he used to know her. And besides, what might not have happened to her in these eight years?

The marriage-pipes sounded, and the mild autumn sun streamed round us. But Rahmun sat in the little Calcutta lane, and saw before him the barren mountains of Afghanistan.

I took out a bank-note, and gave it to him, saying: "Go back to your own daughter, Rahmun, in your own country, and may the happiness of your meeting bring good fortune to my child!"

Having made this present, I had to curtail some of the festivities. I could not have the electric lights I had intended, nor the military band, and the ladies of the house were despondent at it. But to me the wedding feast was all the brighter for the thought that in a distant land a long-lost father met again with his only child.

Exercise

Kabuliwala is a touching short story that tells the heartwarming tale of a fruit seller from Kabul and his inexplicable bond with a little girl named Mini in Kolkata. Through themes of friendship, separation, and parental love, the story beautifully portrays human emotions that go beyond borders and cultures.

I. Narrate your childhood experience with your grandparents or your memories from childhood.

II. Write an imaginative letter from Kabuliwala in jail to his daughter in Afghanistan.

It should include:

- His experiences in India
- His memories of Mini
- His hopes and dreams of reunion with his daughter

III. Who is the narrator of the story Kabuliwala? Find out the difference between first Person narrative and third person narrative.

The Princess and the God: A Tale of Ancient India

Aaron Shepard

In India, in the time of legend, there lived a king with many wives but not one child. Morning and evening for eighteen years, he faced the fire on the sacred altar and prayed for the gift of children.

Finally, a shining goddess rose from the flames.

"I am Savitri, child of the Sun. By your prayers, you have won a daughter."

Within a year, a daughter came to the king and his favorite wife. He named her Savitri, after the goddess.

Beauty and intelligence were the princess Savitri's, and eyes that shone like the sun. So splendid was she, people thought she herself was a goddess. Yet, when the time came for her to marry, no man asked for her.

Her father told her, "Weak men turn away from radiance like yours. Go out and find a man worthy of you. Then I will arrange the marriage."

In the company of servants and councillors, Savitri traveled from place to place. After many days, she came upon a hermitage by a river crossing. Here lived many who had left the towns and cities for a life of prayer and study.

Savitri entered the hall of worship and bowed to the eldest teacher. As they spoke, a young man with shining eyes came into the hall. He guided another man, old and blind.

"Who is that young man?" asked Savitri softly.

"That is Prince Satyavan," said the teacher, with a smile. "He guides his father, a king whose realm was conquered. It is well that Satyavan's name means 'Son of Truth,' for no man is richer in virtue."

When Savitri returned home, she found her father sitting with the holy seer named Narada.

"Daughter," said the king, "have you found a man you wish to marry?"

"Yes, father. His name is Satyavan."

Narada gasped. "Not Satyavan! Princess, no man could be more worthy, but you must not marry him! I know the future. Satyavan will die, one year from today."

The king said, "Do you hear, daughter? Choose a different husband!"

Savitri trembled but said, "I have chosen Satyavan, and I will not choose another. However long or short his life, I wish to share it."

Soon the king rode with Savitri to arrange the marriage.

Satyavan was overjoyed to be offered such a bride. But his father, the blind king, asked Savitri, "Can you bear the hard life of the hermitage? Will you wear our simple robe and our coat of matted bark? Will you eat only fruit and plants of the wild?"

Savitri said, "I care nothing about comfort or hardship. In palace or in hermitage, I am content."

That very day, Savitri and Satyavan walked hand in hand around the sacred fire in the hall of worship. In front of all the priests and hermits, they became husband and wife.

* * *

For a year, they lived happily. But Savitri could never forget that Satyavan's death drew closer.

Finally, only three days remained. Savitri entered the hall of worship and faced the sacred fire. There she prayed for three days and nights, not eating or sleeping.

"My love," said Satyavan, "prayer and fasting are good. But why be this hard on yourself?"

Savitri gave no answer.

The sun was just rising when Savitri at last left the hall. She saw Satyavan heading for the forest, an ax on his shoulder.

Savitri rushed to his side. "I will come with you."

"Stay here, my love," said Satyavan. "You should eat and rest."

But Savitri said, "My heart is set on going."

Hand in hand, Savitri and Satyavan walked over wooded hills. They smelled the blossoms on flowering trees and paused beside clear streams. The cries of peacocks echoed through the woods.

While Savitri rested, Satyavan chopped firewood from a fallen tree. Suddenly, he dropped his ax.

"My head aches."

Savitri rushed to him. She laid him down in the shade of a tree, his head on her lap.

"My body is burning! What is wrong with me?"

Satyavan's eyes closed. His breathing slowed.

Savitri looked up. Coming through the woods to meet them was a princely man. He shone, though his skin was darker than the darkest night. His eyes and his robe were the red of blood.

Trembling, Savitri asked, "Who are you?"

A deep, gentle voice replied. "Princess, you see me only by the power of your prayer and fasting. I am Yama, god of death. Now is the time I must take the spirit of Satyavan."

Yama took a small noose and passed it through Satyavan's breast, as if through air. He drew out a tiny likeness of Satyavan, no bigger than a thumb.

Satyavan's breathing stopped.

Yama placed the likeness inside his robe. "Happiness awaits your husband in my kingdom. Satyavan is a man of great virtue."

Then Yama turned and headed south, back to his domain.

Savitri rose and started after.

Yama strode smoothly and swiftly through the woods, while Savitri struggled to keep up. At last, he stopped to face her.

"Savitri! You cannot follow to the land of the dead!"

"Lord Yama, I know your duty is to take my husband. But my duty as his wife is to stay beside him."

"Princess, that duty is at an end. Still, I admire your loyalty. I will grant you a favor—anything but the life of your husband."

Savitri said, "Please restore my father-in-law's kingdom and his sight."

"His sight and his kingdom shall be restored."

Yama again headed south. Savitri followed.

Along a river bank, thorns and tall, sharp grass let Yama pass untouched. But they tore at Savitri's clothes and skin.

"Savitri! You have come far enough!"

"Lord Yama, I know my husband will find happiness in your kingdom. But you carry away the happiness that is mine!"

"Princess, even love must bend to fate! Still, I admire your devotion. I will grant you another favor—anything but the life of your husband."

Savitri said, "Grant many more children to my father."

"Your father shall have many more children."

Yama once more turned south. Again, Savitri followed.

Up a steep hill Yama glided, while Savitri clambered after him. At the top, he halted.

"Savitri! I forbid you to come farther!"

"Lord Yama, you are respected and revered by all. Yet, no matter what may come, I will remain by Satyavan!"

"Princess, I tell you for the last time, you will not! Still, I can only admire your courage and your firmness. I will grant you one last favor—anything but the life of your husband."

"Then grant many children to me. And let them be children of Satyavan!"

Yama's eyes grew wide as he stared at Savitri. "You did not ask for your husband's life, yet I cannot grant your wish without releasing him. Princess! Your wit is as strong as your will."

Yama took out the spirit of Satyavan and removed the noose. The spirit flew north, quickly vanishing from sight.

"Return, Savitri. You have won your husband's life."

The sun was just setting when Savitri again laid Satyavan's head in her lap.

His chest rose and fell. His eyes opened.

"Is the day already gone? I have slept long. But what is wrong, my love? You smile and cry at the same time!"

"My love," said Savitri, "let us return home."

* * *

Yama was true to all he had promised. Savitri's father became father to many more. Satyavan's father regained both sight and kingdom.

In time, Satyavan became king, and Savitri his queen. They lived long and happily, blessed with many children. So, they had no fear or tears when Yama came again to carry them to his kingdom.

Exercise

The Princess and the God, a tale retold by Aaron Shepard, is the story of Princess Savitri who marries Satyavan, a prince prophesied to die within a year. Despite this, Savitri chooses him, and when Yama, the god of death, comes for Satyavan, Savitri's unwavering love and cleverness lead her to negotiate for his life. Through her wise pleas, she secures not only Satyavan life but also the restoration of his father's sight and kingdom, and the promise of noble descendants. The story, rooted in Hindu mythology, emphasizes themes of love, devotion, and the triumph of good over fate.

I. Analyse critically the portrayal of women in media: Newspapers, Magazines, Radio, Television, Advertisements and Films.

II. Interview a woman who has braved all odds to be successful in a Profession, Entrepreneurship, Public administration or as a homemaker.

III. **Trace the Story Line**

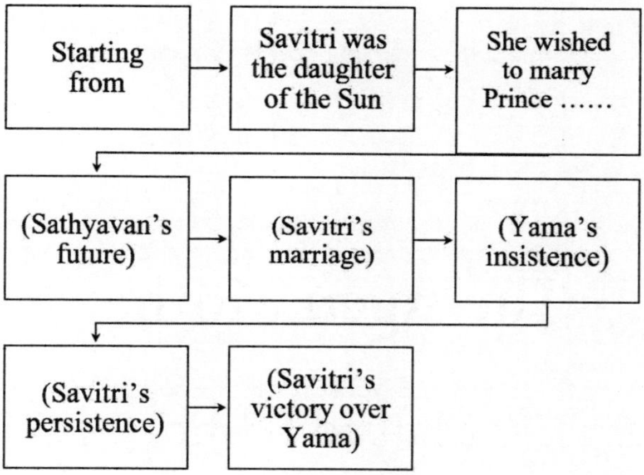

The Aged Mother

Matsuo Basho

Long, long ago there lived at the foot of the mountain a poor farmer and his aged, widowed mother. They owned a bit of land which supplied them with food, and they were humble, peaceful, and happy.

Shining was governed by a despotic leader who though a warrior, had a great and cowardly shrinking from anything suggestive of failing health and strength. This caused him to send out a cruel proclamation. The entire province was given strict orders to immediately put to death all aged people. Those were barbarous days, and the custom of abandoning old people to die was not uncommon. The poor farmer loved his aged mother with tender reverence, and the order filled his heart with sorrow. But no one ever thought twice about obeying the mandate of the governor, so with many deep and hopeless sighs, the youth prepared for what at that time was considered the kindest mode of death.

Just at sundown, when his day's work was ended, he took a quantity of unwhitened rice which was the principal food for the poor, and he cooked, dried it, and tied it in a square cloth, which he swung in a bundle around his neck along with a gourd filled with cool, sweet water. Then he lifted his helpless old mother to his back and started on his painful journey up the mountain. The road was long and steep; the narrow road was crossed and re-crossed by many paths made by the hunters and woodcutters. In some place, they lost and confues, but he gave no heed. One path or another, it mattered not. On he went, climbing blindly upward -- ever upward towards the high bare summit of what is known as Obatsuyama, the mountain of the "abandoning of the aged."

The eyes of the old mother were not so dim but that they noted the reckless hastening from one path to another, and her loving heart grew anxious. Her son did not know the mountain's many paths and his return might be one of danger, so she stretched forth her hand and snapping the twigs from brushes as they passed, she quietly dropped a handful every few steps of the way so that as they climbed, the narrow path behind them was dotted at frequent intervals with tiny piles of twigs. At last the summit was reached. Weary and heart sick, the youth gently released his burden and silently prepared a place of comfort as his last duty to the loved one. Gathering fallen pine needles, he made a soft cushion and tenderly lifted his old mother onto it. Hew rapped her padded coat more closely about the stooping shoulders and with tearful eyes and an aching heart he said farewell.

The trembling mother's voice was full of unselfish love as she gave her last injunction. "Let not thine eyes be blinded, my son." She said. "The mountain road is full of dangers. LOOK carefully and follow the path which holds the piles of twigs. They will guide you to the familiar path farther down." The son's surprised eyes looked back over the path, then at the poor old, shriveled hands all scratched and soiled by their work of love. His heart broke within and bowing to the ground, he cried aloud: "oh, Honorable mother, your kindness breaks my heart! I will not leave you. Together we will follow the path of twigs, and together we will die!"

Once more he shouldered his burden (how light it seemed now) and hastened down the path, through the shadows and the moonlight, to the little hut in the valley. Beneath the kitchen floor was a walled closet for food, which was covered and hidden from view. There the son hid his mother, supplying her with everything she needed, continually watching and fearing she would be discovered. Time passed, and he was beginning to feel safe when again the governor sent forth heralds bearing an unreasonable order, seemingly as a boast of his power. His demand was that his subjects should present him with a rope of ashes.

The entire province trembled with dread. The order must be obeyed yet who in all Shining could make a rope of ashes? One night, in great distress, the son whispered the news to his hidden mother. "Wait!" she said. "I will think. I will think" On the second day she told him what to do. "Make rope of twisted straw," she said. "Then stretch it upon a row of flat stones and burn it on a windless night." He called the people together and did as she said and when the blaze died down, there upon the stones, with every twist and fiber showing perfectly, lay a rope of ashes.

The governor was pleased at the wit of the youth and praised greatly, but he demanded to know where he had obtained his wisdom. "Alas! Alas!" cried the farmer, "the truth must be told!" and with deep bows he related his story. The governor listened and then meditated in silence. Finally he lifted his head. "Shining needs more than strength of youth," he said gravely. "Ah, that I should have forgotten the well-known saying, "with the crown of snow, there cometh wisdom!" That very hour the cruel law was abolished, and custom drifted into as far a past that only legends remain.

Exercise

"The Aged Mother" by Matsuo Bashō is a poignant Japanese folktale that highlights the enduring bond between a mother and her son, set against the backdrop of a ruler's harsh decree. Through a simple yet powerful narrative, the story celebrates wisdom born of age, the strength of compassion, and the quiet heroism of filial love. It gently reminds us that true strength often lies in kindness—and that the old, though frail in body, carry the wisdom that shapes the future.

I. Describe the unique characteristics of your mother and state why she is the best.
II. Write about the poetic forms called "haikai no renga" and "haiku".
III. Illustrate some of the Acts, Parts and Schedules from the Constitution of India those state the Rights of the Elderly.

The Quality of Mercy
(Trial Scene from *The Merchant of Venice*)

William Shakespeare

Act 4, Scene 1

Enter the Duke, the Magnificoes, Antonio, Bassanio, Salerio, and Gratiano, with Attendants.

DUKE What, is Antonio here?
ANTONIO Ready, so please your Grace.
DUKE
I am sorry for thee. Thou art come to answer
A stony adversary, an inhuman wretch,
Uncapable of pity, void and empty
From any dram of mercy.
ANTONIO
I have heard
Your Grace hath ta'en great pains to qualify
His rigorous course; but since he stands obdurate,
And that no lawful means can carry me
Out of his envy's reach, I do oppose
My patience to his fury, and am armed

To suffer with a quietness of spirit
The very tyranny and rage of his.

Duke Go, one, and call the Jew into the court.

Salerio He is ready at the door. He comes, my lord.

Enter Shylock.

Duke

Make room, and let him stand before our face.—
Shylock, the world thinks, and I think so too,
That thou but leadest this fashion of thy malice
To the last hour of act, and then, 'tis thought,
Thou 'lt show thy mercy and remorse more strange
Than is thy strange apparent cruelty;
And where thou now exacts the penalty,
Which is a pound of this poor merchant's flesh,
Thou wilt not only loose the forfeiture,
But, touched with humane gentleness and love,
Forgive a moi'ty of the principal,
Glancing an eye of pity on his losses
That have of late so huddled on his back,
Enow to press a royal merchant down
And pluck commiseration of his state
From brassy bosoms and rough hearts of flint,
From stubborn Turks, and Tartars never trained
To offices of tender courtesy.
We all expect a gentle answer, Jew.

Shylock

I have possessed your Grace of what I purpose,
And by our holy Sabbath have I sworn
To have the due and forfeit of my bond.
If you deny it, let the danger light
Upon your charter and your city's freedom!
You'll ask me why I rather choose to have
A weight of carrion flesh than to receive
Three thousand ducats. I'll not answer that,
But say it is my humor. Is it answered?
What if my house be troubled with a rat,
And I be pleased to give ten thousand ducats

To have it baned? What, are you answered yet?
Some men there are love not a gaping pig,
Some that are mad if they behold a cat,
And others, when the bagpipe sings i' th' nose,
Cannot contain their urine; for affection
Masters oft passion, sways it to the mood
Of what it likes or loathes. Now for your answer:
As there is no firm reason to be rendered
Why he cannot abide a gaping pig,
Why he a harmless necessary cat,
Why he a woolen bagpipe, but of force
Must yield to such inevitable shame
As to offend, himself being offended,
So can I give no reason, nor I will not,
More than a lodged hate and a certain loathing
I bear Antonio, that I follow thus
A losing suit against him. Are you answered?

Bassanio
This is no answer, thou unfeeling man,
To excuse the current of thy cruelty.

Shylock I am not bound to please thee with my answers.
Bassanio Do all men kill the things they do not love?
Shylock Hates any man the thing he would not kill?
Bassanio Every offence is not a hate at first.
Shylock What, wouldst thou have a serpent sting thee twice?

Antonio, *to Bassanio*
I pray you, think you question with the Jew.
You may as well go stand upon the beach
And bid the main flood bate his usual height;
You may as well use question with the wolf
Why he hath made the ewe bleat for the lamb;
You may as well forbid the mountain pines
To wag their high tops and to make no noise
When they are fretten with the gusts of heaven;
You may as well do anything most hard
As seek to soften that than which what's harder?—
His Jewish heart. Therefore I do beseech you

Make no more offers, use no farther means,
But with all brief and plain conveniency
Let me have judgment and the Jew his will.

Bassanio For thy three thousand ducats here is six.

Shylock
If every ducat in six thousand ducats
Were in six parts, and every part a ducat,
I would not draw them. I would have my bond.

Duke How shalt thou hope for mercy, rend'ring none?

Shylock
What judgment shall I dread, doing no wrong?
You have among you many a purchased slave,
Which, like your asses and your dogs and mules,
You use in abject and in slavish parts
Because you bought them. Shall I say to you
"Let them be free! Marry them to your heirs!
Why sweat they under burdens? Let their beds
Be made as soft as yours, and let their palates
Be seasoned with such viands"? You will answer
"The slaves are ours!" So do I answer you:
The pound of flesh which I demand of him
Is dearly bought; 'tis mine and I will have it.
If you deny me, fie upon your law:
There is no force in the decrees of Venice.
I stand for judgment. Answer: shall I have it?

Duke
Upon my power I may dismiss this court
Unless Bellario, a learnèd doctor
Whom I have sent for to determine this,
Come here today.

Salerio
My lord, here stays without
A messenger with letters from the doctor,
New come from Padua.

Duke Bring us the letters. Call the messenger.

Bassanio
Good cheer, Antonio! What, man, courage yet!

The Jew shall have my flesh, blood, bones, and all
Ere thou shalt lose for me one drop of blood!

Antonio

I am a tainted wether of the flock,
Meetest for death. The weakest kind of fruit
Drops earliest to the ground, and so let me.
You cannot better be employed, Bassanio,
Than to live still and write mine epitaph.

Enter Nerissa, disguised as a lawyer's clerk.

Duke Came you from Padua, from Bellario?

Nerissa, *as Clerk*

From both, my lord. Bellario greets your Grace.
Handing him a paper, which he reads, aside, while
Shylock sharpens his knife on the sole of his shoe.

Bassanio Why dost thou whet thy knife so earnestly?

Shylock To cut the forfeiture from that bankrout there.

Gratiano

Not on thy sole but on thy soul, harsh Jew,
Thou mak'st thy knife keen. But no metal can,
No, not the hangman's axe, bear half the keenness
Of thy sharp envy. Can no prayers pierce thee?

Shylock No, none that thou hast wit enough to make.

Gratiano

O, be thou damned, inexecrable dog,
And for thy life let justice be accused;
Thou almost mak'st me waver in my faith,
To hold opinion with Pythagoras
That souls of animals infuse themselves
Into the trunks of men. Thy currish spirit
Governed a wolf who, hanged for human slaughter,
Even from the gallows did his fell soul fleet,
And whilst thou layest in thy unhallowed dam,
Infused itself in thee, for thy desires
Are wolfish, bloody, starved, and ravenous.

Shylock

Till thou canst rail the seal from off my bond,
Thou but offend'st thy lungs to speak so loud.

Repair thy wit, good youth, or it will fall
To cureless ruin. I stand here for law.

Duke

This letter from Bellario doth commend
A young and learnèd doctor to our court.
Where is he?

Nerissa, *as Clerk*

He attendeth here hard by
To know your answer whether you'll admit him.

Duke

With all my heart.—Some three or four of you
Go give him courteous conduct to this place.
Attendants exit.
Meantime the court shall hear Bellario's letter.

Your Grace shall understand that, at the receipt of your letter, I am very sick, but in the instant that your messenger came, in loving visitation was with me a young doctor of Rome. His name is Balthazar. I acquainted him with the cause in controversy between the Jew and Antonio the merchant. We turned o'er many books together. He is furnished with my opinion, which, bettered with his own learning (the greatness whereof I cannot enough commend), comes with him at my importunity to fill up your Grace's request in my stead. I beseech you let his lack of years be no impediment to let him lack a reverend estimation, for I never knew so young a body with so old a head. I leave him to your gracious acceptance, whose trial shall better publish his commendation.

You hear the learnèd Bellario what he writes.
Enter Portia for Balthazar, disguised as a doctor of laws, with Attendants.
And here I take it is the doctor come.—
Give me your hand. Come you from old Bellario?

Portia, *as Balthazar*

I did, my lord.

Duke

You are welcome. Take your place.
Are you acquainted with the difference

That holds this present question in the court?
Portia, *as Balthazar*
I am informèd throughly of the cause.
Which is the merchant here? And which the Jew?
Duke Antonio and old Shylock, both stand forth.
Portia, *as Balthazar*
Is your name Shylock?
Shylock Shylock is my name.
Portia, *as Balthazar*
Of a strange nature is the suit you follow,
Yet in such rule that the Venetian law
Cannot impugn you as you do proceed.
To Antonio. You stand within his danger, do you not?
Antonio Ay, so he says.
Portia, *as Balthazar* Do you confess the bond?
Antonio I do.
Portia, *as Balthazar* Then must the Jew be merciful.
Shylock On what compulsion must I? Tell me that.
Portia, *as Balthazar*
The quality of mercy is not strained.
It droppeth as the gentle rain from heaven
Upon the place beneath. It is twice blest:
It blesseth him that gives and him that takes.
'Tis mightiest in the mightiest; it becomes
The thronèd monarch better than his crown.
His scepter shows the force of temporal power,
The attribute to awe and majesty
Wherein doth sit the dread and fear of kings;
But mercy is above this sceptered sway.
It is enthronèd in the hearts of kings;
It is an attribute to God Himself;
And earthly power doth then show likest God's
When mercy seasons justice. Therefore, Jew,
Though justice be thy plea, consider this:
That in the course of justice none of us
Should see salvation. We do pray for mercy,
And that same prayer doth teach us all to render

The deeds of mercy. I have spoke thus much
To mitigate the justice of thy plea,
Which, if thou follow, this strict court of Venice
Must needs give sentence 'gainst the merchant there.

Shylock
My deeds upon my head! I crave the law,
The penalty and forfeit of my bond.

Portia, *as Balthazar*
Is he not able to discharge the money?

Bassanio
Yes. Here I tender it for him in the court,
Yea, twice the sum. If that will not suffice,
I will be bound to pay it ten times o'er
On forfeit of my hands, my head, my heart.
If this will not suffice, it must appear
That malice bears down truth. *To the Duke.* And I beseech you,
Wrest once the law to your authority.
To do a great right, do a little wrong,
And curb this cruel devil of his will.

Portia, *as Balthazar*
It must not be. There is no power in Venice
Can alter a decree establishèd;
'Twill be recorded for a precedent
And many an error by the same example
Will rush into the state. It cannot be.

Shylock
A Daniel come to judgment! Yea, a Daniel.
O wise young judge, how I do honor thee!

Portia, *as Balthazar*
I pray you let me look upon the bond.

Shylock
Here 'tis, most reverend doctor, here it is.

Handing Portia a paper.

Portia, *as Balthazar*
Shylock, there's thrice thy money offered thee.

Shylock
An oath, an oath, I have an oath in heaven!
Shall I lay perjury upon my soul?
No, not for Venice!

Portia, *as Balthazar*
Why, this bond is forfeit,
And lawfully by this the Jew may claim
A pound of flesh, to be by him cut off
Nearest the merchant's heart.—Be merciful;
Take thrice thy money; bid me tear the bond.

Shylock
When it is paid according to the tenor.
It doth appear you are a worthy judge;
You know the law; your exposition
Hath been most sound. I charge you by the law,
Whereof you are a well-deserving pillar,
Proceed to judgment. By my soul I swear
There is no power in the tongue of man
To alter me. I stay here on my bond.

Antonio
Most heartily I do beseech the court
To give the judgment.

Portia, *as Balthazar* Why, then, thus it is:
You must prepare your bosom for his knife—

Shylock O noble judge! O excellent young man!

Portia, *as Balthazar*
For the intent and purpose of the law
Hath full relation to the penalty,
Which here appeareth due upon the bond.

Shylock
'Tis very true. O wise and upright judge,
How much more elder art thou than thy looks!

Portia, *as Balthazar, to Antonio*
Therefore lay bare your bosom—

Shylock Ay, his breast!
So says the bond, doth it not, noble judge?
"Nearest his heart." Those are the very words.

Portia, *as Balthazar*
It is so.
Are there balance here to weigh the flesh?
Shylock I have them ready.
Portia, *as Balthazar*
Have by some surgeon, Shylock, on your charge,
To stop his wounds, lest he do bleed to death.
Shylock Is it so nominated in the bond?
Portia, *as Balthazar*
It is not so expressed, but what of that?
'Twere good you do so much for charity.
Shylock I cannot find it. 'Tis not in the bond.
Portia, *as Balthazar*
You, merchant, have you anything to say?
Antonio
But little. I am armed and well prepared.—
Give me your hand, Bassanio. Fare you well.
Grieve not that I am fall'n to this for you,
For herein Fortune shows herself more kind
Than is her custom: it is still her use
To let the wretched man outlive his wealth,
To view with hollow eye and wrinkled brow
An age of poverty, from which ling'ring penance
Of such misery doth she cut me off.
Commend me to your honorable wife,
Tell her the process of Antonio's end,
Say how I loved you, speak me fair in death,
And when the tale is told, bid her be judge
Whether Bassanio had not once a love.
Repent but you that you shall lose your friend
And he repents not that he pays your debt.
For if the Jew do cut but deep enough,
I'll pay it instantly with all my heart.
Bassanio
Antonio, I am married to a wife
Which is as dear to me as life itself,
But life itself, my wife, and all the world

Are not with me esteemed above thy life.
I would lose all, ay, sacrifice them all
Here to this devil, to deliver you.

Portia, *aside*

Your wife would give you little thanks for that
If she were by to hear you make the offer.

Gratiano

I have a wife who I protest I love.
I would she were in heaven, so she could
Entreat some power to change this currish Jew.

Nerissa, *aside*

'Tis well you offer it behind her back.
The wish would make else an unquiet house.

Shylock

These be the Christian husbands! I have a
daughter—
Would any of the stock of Barabbas
Had been her husband, rather than a Christian!
We trifle time. I pray thee, pursue sentence.

Portia, *as Balthazar*

A pound of that same merchant's flesh is thine:
The court awards it, and the law doth give it.

Shylock Most rightful judge!

Portia, *as Balthazar*

And you must cut this flesh from off his breast:
The law allows it, and the court awards it.

Shylock Most learnèd judge! A sentence!—Come, prepare.

Portia, *as Balthazar*

Tarry a little. There is something else.
This bond doth give thee here no jot of blood.
The words expressly are "a pound of flesh."
Take then thy bond, take thou thy pound of flesh,
But in the cutting it, if thou dost shed
One drop of Christian blood, thy lands and goods
Are by the laws of Venice confiscate
Unto the state of Venice.

Gratiano O upright judge!—Mark, Jew.—O learnèd judge!

SHYLOCK Is that the law?

PORTIA, *as Balthazar* Thyself shalt see the act.
For, as thou urgest justice, be assured
Thou shalt have justice more than thou desir'st.

GRATIANO O learnèd judge!—Mark, Jew, a learnèd judge!

SHYLOCK
I take this offer then. Pay the bond thrice
And let the Christian go.

BASSANIO Here is the money.

PORTIA, *as Balthazar*
Soft! The Jew shall have all justice. Soft, no haste!
He shall have nothing but the penalty.

GRATIANO O Jew, an upright judge, a learnèd judge!

PORTIA, *as Balthazar*
Therefore prepare thee to cut off the flesh.
Shed thou no blood, nor cut thou less nor more
But just a pound of flesh. If thou tak'st more
Or less than a just pound, be it but so much
As makes it light or heavy in the substance
Or the division of the twentieth part
Of one poor scruple—nay, if the scale do turn
But in the estimation of a hair,
Thou diest, and all thy goods are confiscate.

GRATIANO
A second Daniel! A Daniel, Jew!
Now, infidel, I have you on the hip.

PORTIA, *as Balthazar*
Why doth the Jew pause? Take thy forfeiture.

SHYLOCK Give me my principal and let me go.

BASSANIO I have it ready for thee. Here it is.

PORTIA, *as Balthazar*
He hath refused it in the open court.
He shall have merely justice and his bond.

GRATIANO
A Daniel still, say I! A second Daniel!—
I thank thee, Jew, for teaching me that word.

SHYLOCK Shall I not have barely my principal?

Portia, *as Balthazar*
Thou shalt have nothing but the forfeiture
To be so taken at thy peril, Jew.
Shylock
Why, then, the devil give him good of it!
I'll stay no longer question.*He begins to exit.*
Portia, *as Balthazar* Tarry, Jew.
The law hath yet another hold on you.
It is enacted in the laws of Venice,
If it be proved against an alien
That by direct or indirect attempts
He seek the life of any citizen,
The party 'gainst the which he doth contrive
Shall seize one half his goods; the other half
Comes to the privy coffer of the state,
And the offender's life lies in the mercy
Of the Duke only, 'gainst all other voice.
In which predicament I say thou stand'st,
For it appears by manifest proceeding
That indirectly, and directly too,
Thou hast contrived against the very life
Of the defendant, and thou hast incurred
The danger formerly by me rehearsed.
Down, therefore, and beg mercy of the Duke.
Gratiano
Beg that thou mayst have leave to hang thyself!
And yet, thy wealth being forfeit to the state,
Thou hast not left the value of a cord;
Therefore thou must be hanged at the state's
charge.
Duke
That thou shalt see the difference of our spirit,
I pardon thee thy life before thou ask it.
For half thy wealth, it is Antonio's;
The other half comes to the general state,
Which humbleness may drive unto a fine.
Portia, *as Balthazar*

Ay, for the state, not for Antonio.

Shylock

Nay, take my life and all. Pardon not that.
You take my house when you do take the prop
That doth sustain my house; you take my life
When you do take the means whereby I live.

Portia, *as Balthazar*

What mercy can you render him, Antonio?

Gratiano A halter gratis, nothing else, for God's sake!

Antonio

So please my lord the Duke and all the court
To quit the fine for one half of his goods,
I am content, so he will let me have
The other half in use, to render it
Upon his death unto the gentleman
That lately stole his daughter.
Two things provided more: that for this favor
He presently become a Christian;
The other, that he do record a gift,
Here in the court, of all he dies possessed
Unto his son Lorenzo and his daughter.

Duke

He shall do this, or else I do recant
The pardon that I late pronouncèd here.

Portia, *as Balthazar*

Art thou contented, Jew? What dost thou say?

Shylock I am content.

Portia, *as Balthazar* Clerk, draw a deed of gift.

Shylock

I pray you give me leave to go from hence.
I am not well. Send the deed after me
And I will sign it.

Duke Get thee gone, but do it.

Gratiano

In christ'ning shalt thou have two godfathers.
Had I been judge, thou shouldst have had ten more,
To bring thee to the gallows, not to the font.

Shylock exits.

Duke, *to Portia as Balthazar*

Sir, I entreat you home with me to dinner.

Portia, *as Balthazar*

I humbly do desire your Grace of pardon.
I must away this night toward Padua,
And it is meet I presently set forth.

Duke

I am sorry that your leisure serves you not.—
Antonio, gratify this gentleman,
For in my mind you are much bound to him.

The Duke and his train exit.

Bassanio, *to Portia as Balthazar*

Most worthy gentleman, I and my friend
Have by your wisdom been this day acquitted
Of grievous penalties, in lieu whereof
Three thousand ducats due unto the Jew
We freely cope your courteous pains withal.

Antonio

And stand indebted, over and above,
In love and service to you evermore.

Portia, *as Balthazar*

He is well paid that is well satisfied,
And I, delivering you, am satisfied,
And therein do account myself well paid.
My mind was never yet more mercenary.
I pray you know me when we meet again.
I wish you well, and so I take my leave.
She begins to exit.

Bassanio

Dear sir, of force I must attempt you further.
Take some remembrance of us as a tribute,
Not as fee. Grant me two things, I pray you:
Not to deny me, and to pardon me.

Portia, *as Balthazar*

You press me far, and therefore I will yield.
Give me your gloves; I'll wear them for your sake—

And for your love I'll take this ring from you.
Do not draw back your hand; I'll take no more,
And you in love shall not deny me this.

BASSANIO
This ring, good sir? Alas, it is a trifle.
I will not shame myself to give you this.

PORTIA, *as Balthazar*
I will have nothing else but only this.
And now methinks I have a mind to it.

BASSANIO
There's more depends on this than on the value.
The dearest ring in Venice will I give you,
And find it out by proclamation.
Only for this, I pray you pardon me.

PORTIA, *as Balthazar*
I see, sir, you are liberal in offers.
You taught me first to beg, and now methinks
You teach me how a beggar should be answered.

BASSANIO
Good sir, this ring was given me by my wife,
And when she put it on, she made me vow
That I should neither sell nor give nor lose it.

PORTIA, *as Balthazar*
That 'scuse serves many men to save their gifts.
And if your wife be not a madwoman,
And know how well I have deserved this ring,
She would not hold out enemy forever
For giving it to me. Well, peace be with you.

Portia and Nerissa exit.

ANTONIO
My Lord Bassanio, let him have the ring.
Let his deservings and my love withal
Be valued 'gainst your wife's commandment.

BASSANIO
Go, Gratiano, run and overtake him.
Give him the ring, and bring him if thou canst
Unto Antonio's house. Away, make haste.

Gratiano exits.
Come, you and I will thither presently,
And in the morning early will we both
Fly toward Belmont.—Come, Antonio.
They exit.

Exercise

The theme of mercy is powerfully portrayed in literature, particularly in William Shakespeare's play The Merchant of Venice. One of the most celebrated speeches in the play is delivered by Portia, in which she reflects deeply on the noble and divine essence of mercy. She emphasises that true mercy cannot be compelled; it flows freely from a generous heart and brings blessings to both the one who gives and the one who receives it. Unlike strict justice, which focuses on punishment, mercy highlights forgiveness and compassion. The speech encourages readers and audiences to recognise the moral strength in choosing kindness over retribution, even when one has the authority to enforce justice. Shakespeare presents mercy as a godlike quality, capable of softening the harshness of law and elevating human behaviour. In a world frequently governed by rules and revenge, mercy is an enduring call for grace, empathy, and understanding.

I. Imagine Portia's speech delivered in a contemporary courtroom setting. Write a scene where a modern-day lawyer argues for mercy, using language and examples relevant to today's world.

Refer to the example given below:

Modern Courtroom – Day

The courtroom is silent. JUDGE MILTON, stern but fair, sits behind the bench. The plaintiff, Mr. Miller, watches coldly. The defendant, Mary Wroth, a single mother accused of embezzling from the company she worked for, sits with her head low.

Her defense attorney, Ruth Godwin, late 30s, professional and composed, stands to deliver closing remarks.

Your Honor, before you render judgment, I ask—not for a dismissal, not for exoneration—but for mercy.

Mercy, unlike justice, asks us to consider more than facts and laws. It asks us to consider humanity. It doesn't excuse wrongdoing, but it invites us to understand it.

The law, at its best, isn't a blunt instrument—it's a framework for fairness. And fairness isn't always found in the harshest penalty.

Mary Wroth is guilty. She admits to taking money. But let's not overlook why. This was not greed; it was desperation. Her son has leukemia. She was drowning in medical debt. She made the wrong choice, yes—but not from malice...

II. Pick up a few phrases from Shakespeare's plays that are commonly used in spoken language today. For example:
   - "All that glitters is not gold" – The Merchant of Venice
   - "Naked truth" – Love's Labour's Lost
   - "Faint-hearted" – Henry VI, Part I
   - "Melted into thin air" – The Tempest
   - "Own flesh and blood" – Hamlet

III. **Argument Writing:** Present your argument asserting your position on a topic you are interested. For example – Can AI replace human teachers? Are Friends better than family?